THE WORKSHOP COMPANION™

ROUTING AND SHAPING

TECHNIQUES FOR BETTER WOODWORKING

by Nick Engler

This paperback edition of *Routing and Shaping*
has been printed exclusively for
Creative Homeowner Press, 24 Park Way, Upper Saddle River, NJ 07458.

Rodale Press
Emmaus, Pennsylvania

Printed in the United States of America
on acid-free ∞, recycled paper ♻

If you have any questions or comments concerning this
book, please write:
Rodale Press
Book Reader Service
33 East Minor Street
Emmaus, PA 18098

About the Author: Nick Engler is an experienced woodworker, writer, and teacher. For many years, he was a
luthier making traditional American musical instruments
before he founded *Hands On!* magazine. Today, he contri-
butes to other how-to magazines and has published over
20 books on the wood arts. He teaches woodworking at
the University of Cincinnati.

Series Editor: Jeff Day
Editors: Roger Yepsen
            Kenneth Burton
Copy Editor: Sarah Dunn
Graphic Designer: Linda Watts
Graphic Artists: Mary Jane Favorite
            Chris Walendzak
Photographer: Karen Callahan
Cover Photographer: Mitch Mandel
Proofreader: Hue Park
Typesetting by Computer Typography, Huber Heights, Ohio
Interior and Endpaper Illustrations by Mary Jane Favorite
Produced by Bookworks, Inc., West Milton, Ohio

Library of Congress Cataloging-in-Publication Data

Engler, Nick.
    Routing and shaping/by Nick Engler.
        p.   cm. — (The workshop companion)
    Includes index.
    ISBN 0–87596–107–X   hardcover
    ISBN 0-87596-610-1 paperback
    1. Routers (Tools) 2. Woodwork. 3. Shapers. I. Title
    II. Series.
TT203.5.E54   1991
684'.083—dc20   91–27328
                                                    CIP

12   14   16   18   20   19   17   15   13   hardcover
    4   6   8   10   9   7   5   3   paperback

Special Thanks to:

Delta International Machinery
    Corporation,
Pittsburgh, Pennsylvania

Wertz Hardware
West Milton, Ohio

Woodworker's Supply of New Mexico
Albuquerque, New Mexico

CONTENTS

TECHNIQUES

PROJECTS

TECHNIQUES

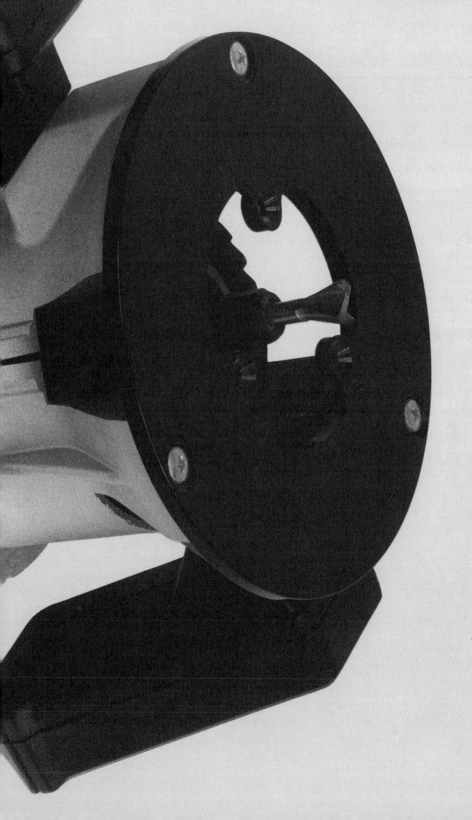

1

USING ROUTERS AND SHAPERS

Ever since men and women started working wood, they have been shaping it. Some of the earliest known examples of wooden furniture — Egyptian and Mesopotamian chests — display shaped surfaces. Ancient craftsmen often repeated simple, pleasing shapes, not only within the design of a single piece but also from piece to piece. We know these recurring shapes as *moldings*.

Over the centuries, woodworkers have used many different tools to duplicate molded shapes. Roman woodworkers developed

molding planes with contoured soles and irons. (*SEE FIGURE 1-1.*) These remained in general use for over two millennia, until the mid-nineteenth century when machine tools with rotary cutters began to replace them. Among these new tools was the *spindle shaper,* a vertical shaft (or spindle) on which cutters of various shapes could be mounted and spun at high speeds. (Contemporary woodworkers have shortened the name to *shaper.*)

In the early twentieth century, during World War I, patternmaker R. L. Carter invented a *portable*

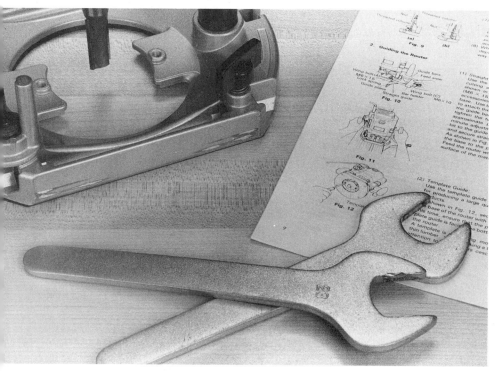

shaper. Carter had been making 16 identical wooden patterns for a large boiler. The patterns were too unwieldy to be cut on a shaper, and this job might have required days of tedious work with a spoke-shave or molding plane. But Carter was short of time. So he cannibalized a barber's electric clippers, removing the motor and worm gear. He reground the gear to make a small roundover cutter and rigged a guide for the tool. Carter was able to shape the pattern edges in about two hours.

After the war, Carter began to manufacture what he called hand shapers for patternmakers, cabinet-makers, and other professional woodworkers. He refined his invention, adding a base, a collet, and interchangeable cutting tools, and termed the improved machine a router. Ten years after the war, when the R. L. Carter Company was producing 100,000 routers a year, Stanley Tools bought them and introduced the router to amateur craftsmen and hobbyists.

Today, routers and shapers have evolved far beyond the simple molding plane. Both professional and amateur woodworkers now use them not only for cutting molded shapes but also for joinery, duplicating, trimming, carving, and dozens of other tasks. Many contemporary woodworking projects would be impossible without them.

ROUTER AND SHAPER ANATOMY

THE BASIC PARTS

Because routers and shapers evolved from the same ancestor, their anatomy is similar. In many ways, the router is just a small version of the shaper. Reduced to its simplest form, each tool is a motor and a shaft with means of holding interchangeable shaper cutters or router bits.

The cutting edges of the bits and cutters are called *flutes*. Most router bits have two symmetrical flutes, although there are a few with just one. (One-flute bits cut slower, provide more clearance for wood chips,

and won't burn the wood as easily.) While most shaper cutters have three flutes, some have as few as two or as many as four. (SEE FIGURE 1-2.) The shape of the flutes determines the shape of the cut — after it's shaped or routed, the wood is the *reverse* of the flute. A cove on a flute becomes a bead on the workpiece. Both routers and shapers spin the bits and cutters at extremely high speeds to produce a smooth surface, no matter what the shape. (SEE FIGURE 1-3.)

1-1 Both the router and the shaper share a common ancestor — the *molding plane*. This hand tool had a contoured sole and a contoured iron to cut a molded shape in the wood surface. Craftsmen usually made their own molding planes, filing the irons and carving the soles to a variety of shapes. A single craftsman often had dozens of molding planes — for the same reason a contemporary woodworker might own dozens of router bits or shaper cutters.

1-2 Both routers and shapers use rotary bits and cutters with one or more *flutes*. Generally, the more flutes on a cutter, the slower it's intended to spin. This is why most router bits, which spin at up to 30,000 rpm, have only two flutes, and most shaper cutters, which travel at less than 10,000 rpm, have three.

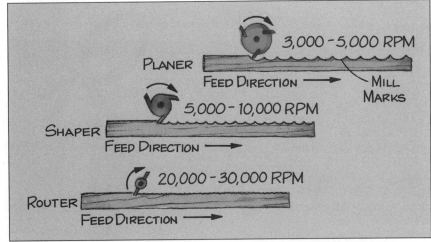

1-3 Low-speed power tools with rotary cutters, such as jointers and planers, leave visible *mill marks* — tiny scallops in the surface of the wood. Routers and shapers leave mill marks, too. But because their

cutters turn at such high speeds, the mill marks are much smaller and more closely spaced. By routing and shaping slowly, you get a high number of cuts per inch, and the mill marks should be almost invisible.

There are important differences, however. Shapers are stationary power tools, while routers are portable. Consequently, they aren't built alike — their controls are dissimilar, and many of the techniques for using them are distinctly different. (*SEE FIGURES 1-4 AND 1-5.*)

As you can see, the shaper is more complex than the router — there are several additional controls and features. But this does not necessarily mean that the shaper will do more. The router, in fact, is more versatile. The shaper's strong suit is its ability to cut large amounts of stock quickly and continuously.

have features in addition to those listed here. Furthermore, shapers and routers of many different sizes and capacities have evolved. There is now a complete routing and shaping spectrum, starting with miniature routers that accept bits with 1/16-inch shanks and continuing up to massive production shapers with 1 1/2-inch spindles.

To fill in the gray area between the two tools, many manufacturers offer special routing spindles for shapers, and spindle accessories for routers. (*SEE FIGURES 1-6 AND 1-7.*) There is even such an animal as a *router/shaper* — a small, bench-top tool that combines features of both tools. (*SEE FIGURE 1-8.*)

WHERE TO FIND IT

You can purchase a shaper spindle accessory for your router from:

Delta Machinery Corporation
246 Alpha Drive
Pittsburgh, PA 15238

Wood Werks Supply, Inc.
372 Morrison Road
Columbus, OH 43213

A SAFETY REMINDER

*O*nly use a shaper spindle router accessory in a router with a *variable speed control* — either a control that has been built into the tool itself, or an external control that you can plug the router into. Set this control for no more than 10,000 rpm — the top speed of many shapers — when using the spindle accessory. Most shaper cutters are designed to operate within shaper speeds, while many routers spin more than twice that fast. At excessive speeds, the cutters may fly apart, peppering you and anyone who happens to be standing nearby with shrapnel.

THE ROUTING AND SHAPING SPECTRUM

This brief anatomy is an oversimplification, of course. Specific types or brands of routers and shapers may

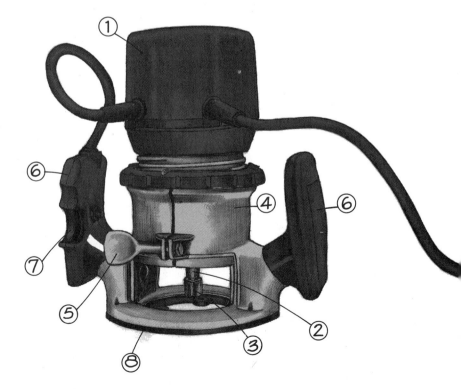

1-4 The bulk of the router is made up by its *motor* (1). An *arbor* (2) protrudes from the bottom of this motor. The end of the arbor is fitted with a *collet* (3) to hold the router bits. The motor, arbor, and collet are mounted in a *base* (4). The base incorporates a *height clamp* (5) to raise or lower the motor, and secure it in that position. A router also has *handles* (6) so it can be guided, and has a nearby *on/off switch* (7). This entire assembly resets on a removable plastic *sole* (8) or base plate.

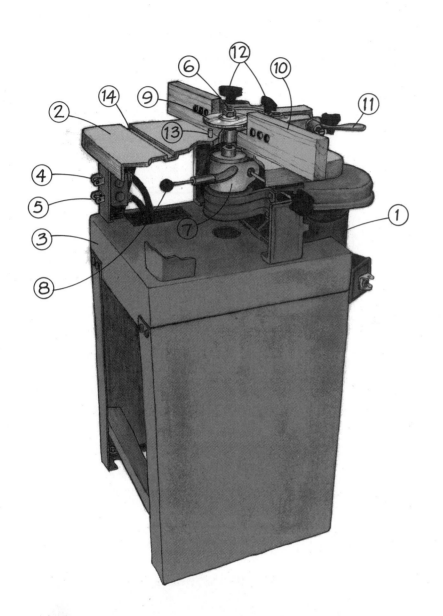

1-6 Many shaper manufacturers make a special *routing spindle* for their machines. This has a collet on the end so you can mount router bits in the shaper. You simply remove the traditional threaded spindle and replace it with the routing spindle.

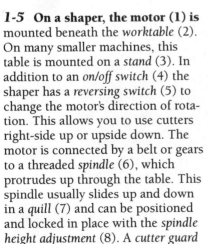

1-7 You can also purchase a threaded *shaper spindle* that will fit in a ½-inch router collet. This enables you to mount small shaper cutters on your router. *However —* and this is an extremely important however — you should *only use these spindles on routers with a variable speed control*. Adjust the speed control to no more than 10,000 rpm. Also, use this accessory *only with the router mounted in a router table* or other stationary jig.

1-5 On a shaper, the motor (1) is mounted beneath the *worktable* (2). On many smaller machines, this table is mounted on a *stand* (3). In addition to an *on/off switch* (4) the shaper has a *reversing switch* (5) to change the motor's direction of rotation. This allows you to use cutters right-side up or upside down. The motor is connected by a belt or gears to a threaded *spindle* (6), which protrudes up through the table. This spindle usually slides up and down in a *quill* (7) and can be positioned and locked in place with the *spindle height adjustment* (8). A *cutter guard* (9) covers the cutter after it's mounted on the spindle. A *split fence* (10) fits around the spindle and guides the workpiece past the cutter. The left and right sides of this fence can be moved independently with the *fence adjustment* (11). On some shapers, the entire fence can be moved as one unit, then secured to the table with *fence clamps* (12). Or the fence can be removed completely so you can use a *starting pin* (13) to help guide the workpiece. A *miter gauge slot* (14) in the table runs parallel to the fence, letting you use miter gauges and sliding jigs to guide the work.

1-8 *Router/shapers* **are hybrid** power tools that combine features of both routers and shapers, notably a slow-speed router motor with a ½-inch threaded shaper spindle (although some have a router arbor and collet instead of a spindle). The motor is mounted in a small shaper table with a split fence. The result is a light-duty bench-top shaper that's almost as easy to move around as a router.

SELECTING A PORTABLE ROUTER
TYPE OF ROUTERS

When you go shopping for a portable router, you'll find they can generally be classified into four categories. (*SEE FIGURE 1-9.*)

■ The *basic router* is simply a motor mounted on a base. Most of these tools offer ½ to 1½ horsepower, and their collets will only accept router bits with ¼-inch shanks. The bases are usually 6 inches in diameter.

■ The *plunge router* does all the things a basic router can do and makes "plunge cuts." The motor is mounted on two spring-loaded slides above the base. This lets you position the motor above the work, push the bit down into the wood, and begin cutting — very handy for making mortises and other interior cuts. Both the motors and the bases on plunge routers tend to be larger than those on basic routers. Many come with interchangeable ½-inch and ¼-inch collets.

■ The *laminate trimmer* is an abridged version of the basic router with a smaller motor and base and has a ¼-inch collet made especially for trimming laminates and veneers. These materials are usually oversized when applied to a surface, and the smaller size of a laminate trimmer makes it easier to control when cutting them to size. It's especially handy when you are balancing the tool on thin or narrow workpieces. It's also useful for many other routing chores that require finesse rather than brute strength. Some trimmers come with interchangeable bases that allow you to work in tight areas or rout at an angle.

1-9 **There are many types of** portable routers, varying in size and capacity. They can be organized into four categories (from left to right): miniature router, laminate trimmer, basic router, and plunge router.

■ The *miniature router* lets you use very small router bits and accessories for delicate work. This is a carving or engraving tool that can be mounted in a router base accessory. It usually has interchangeable collets that accept bits with $\frac{1}{16}$- and $\frac{1}{8}$-inch shanks. The small size allows you to rout inlays, cut mortises for small hardware, make delicate joints, and perform other jobs where a standard-size router or even a laminate trimmer would be too clumsy.

ROUTER FEATURES AND CAPABILITIES

Once you narrow the field to the type of router you need, consider the capabilities of the tools in that category. Here are several important features to consider:

Collet — If every tool has its Achilles' heel, then the router's is the collet. Although the collet seems small and insignificant, it's a critical part. A poorly designed collet may let the bit slip, ruining the cut. To compensate, many craftsmen overtighten the collet, which only aggravates the problem. Overtightening makes the bits hard to mount and dismount and causes excessive wear.

To avoid the vexation, get a router with a good collet. You can judge whether a collet will give you problems by considering how it works. A collet is a split or segmented collar at the end of the arbor that holds the shank of the router bit. Tightening a nut squeezes the collar around the shank, locking the bit in place. Generally, the more segments on a collet, the better. These make the collet more flexible so it can get a better grip on the bit shank. *(SEE FIGURE 1-10.)* Routers with multiple-segment collets tend to be more expensive, but the potential headaches they eliminate are well worth the expense.

Note: Some routers have split arbors rather than collets. But the same rule applies — the more segments, the better.

In addition to the design of the collet, also consider the size. Collets come in three sizes — $\frac{1}{4}$, $\frac{3}{8}$, and $\frac{1}{2}$ inch (inside diameter). Most off-the-shelf router bits have $\frac{1}{4}$-inch shanks, but there is a wider variety of $\frac{1}{2}$-inch bits available through mail-order suppliers. Also, $\frac{1}{2}$-inch bits run truer and are more durable. In addition, a few useful specialty bits have $\frac{3}{8}$-inch shanks. If you want to take full advantage of all the bits that are available to you, choose a router with interchangeable collets.

Note: Some routers only have $\frac{1}{2}$-inch collets, but come with split bushing so you can adapt them to hold $\frac{1}{4}$- and $\frac{3}{8}$-inch bits. This is okay, but not as desirable as interchangeable collets.

Power — The type of woodworking you want to do with the router will determine the horsepower you need. If you're buying the router just to make a few occasional moldings and joints, 1 horsepower will be more than sufficient. On the other hand, if you expect to do a lot of routing or if you want to use bits with large flute diameters, then you should look at 2- and 3-horsepower models.

Speed — Along with power, consider speed. Most single-speed routers operate between 20,000 and 30,000 rpm. This is adequate for bits with flute diameters of 2 inches or less. But larger bits should run at slower speeds; otherwise, they'll overheat and burn the wood. If you intend to use large bits often or want to use the shaper spindle accessory mentioned earlier, invest in some method of varying the speed of the motor, such as an internal, built-in speed control or an external, in-line controller. *(SEE FIGURE 1-11.)*

Note: There are two types of speed controllers — simple rheostats and electronic speed controllers. Rheostats simply reduce the line voltage, which lowers both the speed and the available torque — the ability of your router to do serious work. As a result,

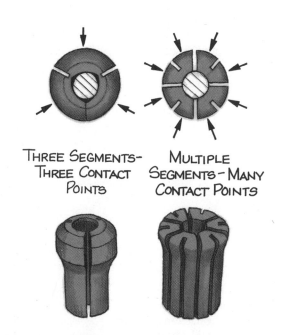

THREE SEGMENTS—
THREE CONTACT
POINTS

MULTIPLE
SEGMENTS—MANY
CONTACT POINTS

1-10 Collets with just two or three segments don't squeeze router bit shanks evenly. In fact, they make contact at just a few points. Collets with multiple segments are more flexible and make contact all the way around the shank. This helps keep the bit from slipping.

the router may bog down when you try to cut. Electronic speed controllers, on the other hand, have a feedback mechanism that boosts the available torque at low speeds. The router is less likely to quit when the going gets tough.

FOR YOUR INFORMATION

Despite a popular misconception, speed controllers will not harm *universal* motors — the type of motor found in all routers and most hand-held power tools. However, they can ruin *induction* motors, such as the capacitor-start motors on many shapers and other stationary power tools. If you purchase an in-line speed controller, use it for your portable power tools *only*.

Height adjustment — Most basic routers can be raised or lowered up to 2 inches. If the work you do requires more movement than this, consider a plunge router — these usually have about half again as much travel. Also consider the ease and accuracy with which you can change the height — here again, plunge routers usually have an advantage over basic routers. Remember, you'll be changing the height constantly, more than any other router adjustment. Make it as easy on yourself as possible.

Note: On some basic routers, the motor housings are threaded in the base so you screw them up or down. This allows you to make minute height changes accurately. But in some respects, the arrangement is a pain in the neck. Since the on/off switch revolves with the motor, you never quite know where it is. And if you mount the router to a router table or other stationary jig, the cord quickly becomes twisted.

Configuration — Consider how the router is put together. Is it too heavy or not heavy enough? Is it well balanced or does it seem top heavy? Can you reach the on/off switch and other essential controls without taking your hands from the handles? Does the base allow you to see what you're cutting? Will the size and shape of the base help you or interfere with your work? (*SEE FIGURE 1-12*.)

Accessories — Finally, give some thought to router accessories. Can you put together the routing *system* you want around a particular router? Will the router work with the accessories you already own? And will the complete system — router *and* accessories — do all the routing chores you need it to?

ADVICE FOR THE NOVICE

Much of the above information is useful only if you already know what kinds of routing tasks you want to perform. But what if you have little or no experience with a router and just want to explore the possibilities?

My advice is to purchase a basic router with ¾ to 1¼ horsepower and a ¼-inch collet. This will perform 90 percent of all home workshop routing tasks and should serve you well for many years, even after you're ready to add more advanced capabilities to your routing system.

1-11 A few routers come with built-in electronic speed controls. (*See inset, upper right.*) You can also purchase an external in-line speed controller that varies the electrical current before it gets to the router. Plug this controller into the wall outlet, then plug the router into the controller. One important advantage of an external controller is that if you have more than one router, you can use this accessory with all of them.

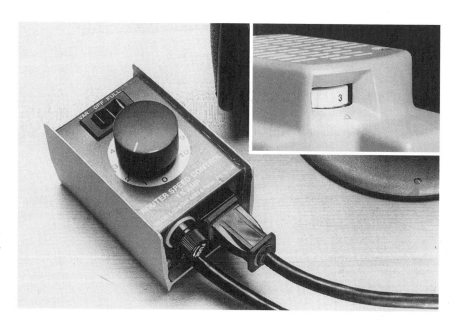

1-12 Router bases come in a variety of sizes and shapes. The round base found on most basic routers (left) is useful for most operations but may be slightly inaccurate when following a straightedge. The plunge router base (middle) has one straight side so you can accurately follow both straight and curved templates. The laminate trimmer (right) has a square base with rounded corners. It not only can follow both straight and curved templates but also can do so no matter how you turn it.

MOUNTING A ROUTER

THREE BASIC POSITIONS

After you've worked with a portable router for some time, you'll find that many operations are easier and safer if you *mount* the router — hold it stationary by attaching it to a table or jig. This enables you to pass the workpiece across the bit instead of the other way around.

There are three common ways to mount a router: vertically beneath the work, vertically above the work, and horizontally beside the work. (*SEE FIGURE 1-13.*) Each position offers some unique advantages, and there are tools and jigs commonly available that will hold the router in each position mentioned.

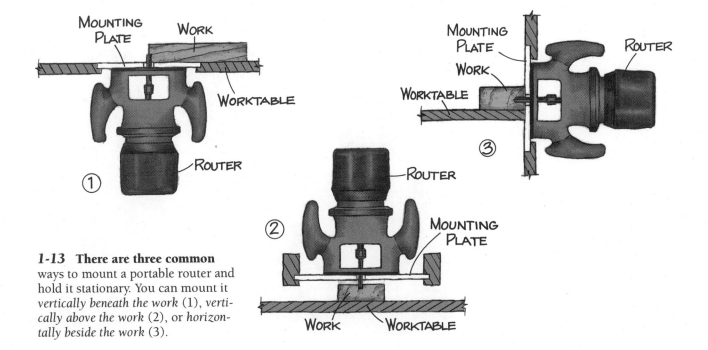

1-13 There are three common ways to mount a portable router and hold it stationary. You can mount it *vertically beneath the work* (1), *vertically above the work* (2), or *horizontally beside the work* (3).

THE ROUTER TABLE

You can purchase or make many different router-mounting jigs and accessories, but the most versatile is the *router table*. This device holds the router vertically beneath the work. The bit protrudes up through the table, as on a shaper. Simply rest the work on the table and guide it over the bit. (*See Figure 1-14.*)

There are many commercial router tables on the market, and several you can make from a kit. But you can easily make your own from scratch. A homemade router table may be better in the long run — you can build it to fit your particular router and to suit the space available in your workshop. Or, if you don't have room for a stand-alone table, you can customize other fixtures that are already in your shop to hold a router. A workbench, a table saw, and a radial arm saw can do double-duty as a router table. (*See Figure 1-15.*)

When you use a router table, make sure that it's stable. If it isn't connected to a cabinet or other shop fixture, clamp it down to your workbench. You may want to add a dust collector — a simple shroud to vacuum the sawdust as you work. (*See Figure 1-16.*) You may also want to install an electrical switch and outlet near the front of the table to turn the router on and off easily. (*See Figure 1-17.*)

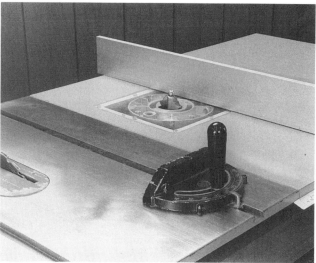

1-15 If you don't have the space for a router table, consider mounting your router in a workbench or another shop fixture. This table saw incorporates a router mount in one of the table extensions. Not only does this provide a large work surface, but you can also use the table saw fence and miter gauge with the router.

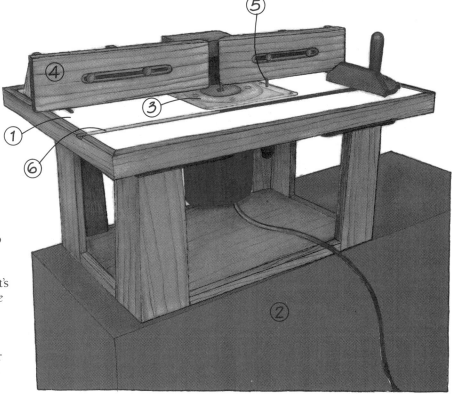

1-14 A router table is a simple but versatile mounting jig, made up of a *worktable* (1) mounted on a *stand* (2). Usually, the router is attached to a *mounting plate* (3) that's mortised into the worktable. A *fence* (4), a *starting pin* (5), and a *miter gauge slot* (6) provide several ways to guide a workpiece over the bit. The design for this particular router table is included in the *Projects* section on page 97.

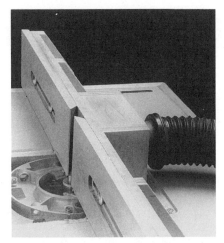

1-16 If possible, make sure your router table includes a dust collector to keep the mess to a minimum as you work. On this table, the collector is part of the fence.

1-17 When a router is mounted in a router table, it may be hard to reach the switch. To solve this problem, mount a combination switch/outlet near the front of the router

table and wire it to control the power to the outlet. Plug your router into the outlet, and use the switch to turn it on and off.

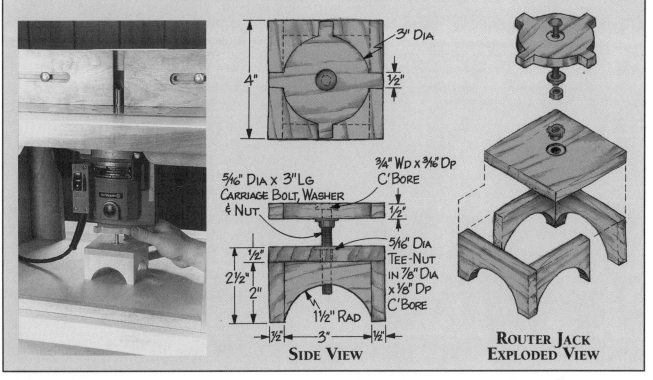

TRY THIS TRICK

One of the most difficult chores to perform on a router table is *accurately* adjusting the height of the bit above the worktable. With the router secured under the table and surrounded by the stand, height adjustment can be a hit-or-miss proposition. But this simple shop-made jig removes the guesswork. It's actually a

small, precise screw jack. Place the wooden plate under the router motor and turn it left or right. This turns a bolt in a T-nut, raising or lowering the plate — *and the motor* — in tiny increments. You can make this as a separate accessory, or incorporate it into the design of your router table.

SIDE VIEW

ROUTER JACK EXPLODED VIEW

MAKING A MOUNTING PLATE

To mount a router in a stationary jig (such as a router table), you must first make a router mounting plate — a thin, flat sheet to which you attach the router base. Then mortise or inset the plate into the work surface of the jig.

Making a mounting plate is straightforward — cut the material to size, drill a few holes, and screw the plate to the jig. However, you must make several informed decisions as you fashion this simple part.

1 **The material from which you** make a mounting plate must be strong enough and dense enough to absorb the vibrations of the router, yet thin enough that it won't restrict the depth of cut. You should also be able to cut and drill the material easily. Finally, the material should be *transparent*, so you can see what's going on beneath it. There is really only one material that fulfills all three requirements — transparent plastic. I suggest you use ordinary, inexpensive acrylic plastic. Some structural plastics, such as Lexan, are super-strong but too flexible. Acrylic is more rigid. Use a 1/4-inch-thick sheet for routers up to 1 1/2 horsepower and a 3/8-inch-thick sheet for more powerful routers.

2 **For safety and accuracy,** there should be as little space as possible between the work surface and the router bit where it protrudes through the mounting plate. However, bits range in size from 1/16 inch to 3 1/4 inch. To accommodate this range, you should drill the opening about 1/4 inch larger than the cutting radius of your largest bit, then fashion several *inserts* to fit the opening. Use the same transparent material that the mounting plate was made from. Drill a different diameter hole in the center of each insert so you have a variety to choose from.

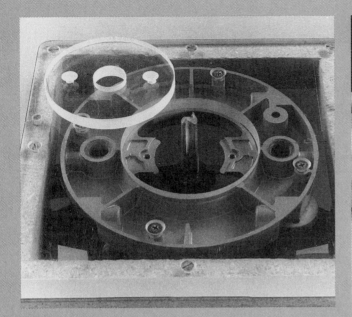

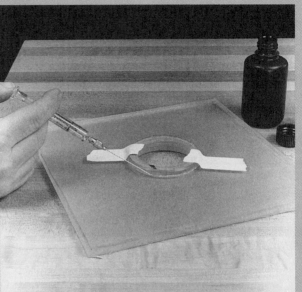

3 **You will also have to fashion** some way to hold the inserts. Some router bases have metal or plastic flanges to mount guide bushings. If your router is so equipped, use these flanges to support and secure the inserts.

4 **If the router base doesn't** have built-in flanges, attach a plastic ring to the underside of the mounting plate. The inside diameter of this ring should be about ¹/₂ inch smaller than the diameter of the mounting plate opening — this will create a ledge to support the inserts. Apply acrylic cement with a syringe, letting it flow between the plastic parts.

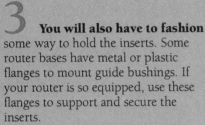

5 **To mortise the jig's work** surface for the mounting plate, first rout a square groove in the surface. Clamp a wooden frame to the jig to guide the router, and cut the groove so the depth matches the thickness of the mounting plate. **Note:** Make this groove about ¹/₃₂ inch smaller than the circumference of the plate. Later, sand or file the edges of the plate to get a perfect fit. You may also want to cut the groove about ¹/₆₄ inch deeper than necessary, then shim the plate with strips of paper or tape until it's perfectly flush with the work surface.

(continued) ▷

MAKING A MOUNTING PLATE — CONTINUED

6 **Make the router opening by** cutting around the inside edges of the groove with a saber saw. When the waste falls away, the groove will form a ledge to hold the mounting plate.

7 **Secure the mounting plate in** the mortise with several screws. Don't leave it loose; it may shift as you work. If it's a small plate (less than 8 inches square), position screws at all four corners. Larger plates should be fastened at the corners *and* midway along the sides — at eight points altogether. Make sure that the heads of the screws used to attach the plate are flush with or slightly below the plate surface.

8 **The work surface should** be thick enough to permit attaching the mounting plate securely — short screws may vibrate or pull loose. If the work surface is less than 1¼ inch thick, build up the area immediately beneath the mounting plate by gluing a hardwood frame to the jig.

THE OVERARM ROUTER

Although a good router table will perform most of the tasks that require a stationary router, there are times when you need to mount the router *over* the work rather than under it. An *overarm router* holds the bit vertically above the work. (*See Figure 1-18.*)

The most obvious advantage to this setup is that you can see what you're cutting. The overarm router also lets you make interior cuts. (*See Figure 1-19.*) And you can rout cylindrical stock, holding the workpiece in an ordinary V-jig. (*See Figure 1-20.*)

1-18 An overarm router works like a stationary plunge router. A long *arm* (1) supports the router above a *worktable* (2). At the end of the arm, a *height adjustment lever* (3) and *height clamp* (4) allow you to change the height of the router quickly and precisely. Finally, most overarm routers have a *pin block* (5) immediately beneath the router to hold guide pins.

1-19 To make an interior cut with an overarm router, simply lower the bit into the wood, make the cut, and retract it. You don't have to worry about cutting through to the outside edge.

1-20 You can also rout dowels and spindle turnings with an over-arm router. To cut flutes, beads, and other designs along the axis of cylindrical workpieces, mount them in a simple V-jig. Guide the V-jig along a fence or straightedge clamped to the worktable.

MAKING AND USING AN OVERHEAD ROUTING JIG

Although an overarm router is a useful tool, it's also expensive. If you have only an occasional need to mount your router above the work, make this *overhead routing jig* — a simple, adjustable platform that holds the router above a workbench. If you mount a plunge router on the jig, it can do almost everything an overarm router can do (although not as quickly or easily).

As you can see by the plans, the jig is straightforward. However, carefully consider the dimensions before you build it. Make the platform as long as possible, but not so long that it flexes under the weight of your router.

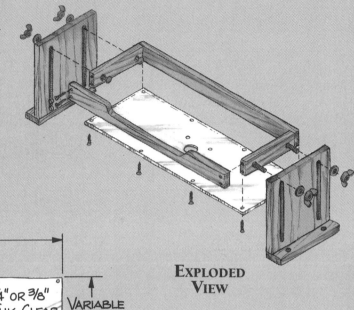

EXPLODED VIEW

MOUNTING PLATE LAYOUT

- VARIABLE UP TO 24"
- 3/8" (TYP)
- 6" (APPROX.)
- 3/16" DIA THRU with C'SINK
- 1/4" OR 3/8" THK CLEAR PLASTIC
- 1" DIA THRU O.C.
- VARIABLE TO FIT ROUTER

NOTE: Mount overhead routing fixture to router table with carriage bolts, washers and wing nuts (4 required), using mounting slots. Or, clamp it to the workbench.

TOP VIEW

- 3/4"
- ROUTER MOUNTING HOLES
- 3/8" DIA HOLES (THRU)
- 1 3/4"

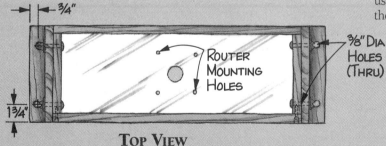

FRONT VIEW

- 1" RAD
- VARIABLE
- 3/8" x 2" CARRIAGE BOLT, WASHER & WING NUT (4 REQ'D)
- 2"
- 3/4" (TYP)
- 1"
- #10 x 1 1/2" FHWS
- 2 1/4"
- 2 1/4"

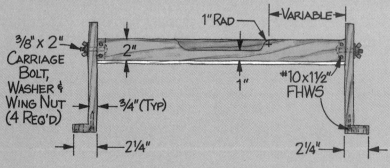

END VIEW

- 1 3/4" (TYP)
- 1"
- 9 1/4"
- 7 1/4"
- 3/8" WD SLOTS
- 3/4"
- VARIABLE
- 1"

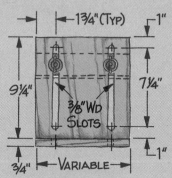

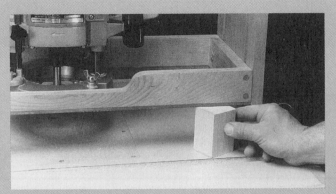

1 **To use the overhead routing** jig, clamp or bolt both legs securely to your workbench. Make coarse height adjustments by raising or lowering the platform, and fine adjustments by raising or lowering the router motor in its base. Check that all four corners of the platform are precisely the same distance off the workbench by checking with a *feeler block,* as shown. If the platform isn't level, the router bit won't be square with the work.

2 **To guide the workpiece** under the jig, clamp a straightedge to the workbench. Use this as you would a fence.

3 **To make a plunge cut with** the jig, you must use a plunge router. Carefully position the workpiece under the bit and clamp it to the workbench. Turn the router on and plunge it into the wood.

4 **Tighten the height clamp on** the router to hold it at the proper height. Let go of the router, loosen the clamps that hold the workpiece, and make the cut. When you've finished, turn the router off and let it come to a complete stop before raising the tool and removing the work. **Note:** A foot switch (offered by many mail-order suppliers) can be a real boon when using this jig. You can turn the router on and off without having to let go of the work.

THE JOINT MAKER

The latest wrinkle in router evolution is the *joint maker,* a tool that mounts a router horizontally beside the work. These machines vary widely in complexity and capability. At the simple end of the scale, some joint makers are nothing more than a worktable and a movable frame on which to mount your router. The more capable machines move the router or the work in several directions and follow templates to reproduce complex joints. *(SEE FIGURES 1-21 AND 1-22.)*

A horizontally mounted router offers several advantages when cutting certain joints. Like the overarm router, the joint maker lets you see your work as you cut it. You can rest the stock flat on the worktable, which gives you more stability when routing edges. And the increased visibility and stability help to make the jig safer for some operations.

If you only have an occasional need for this accessory, these advantages may not be enough to justify the expense. However, you can easily build a simple, inexpensive joint maker. Plans for a joint-making jig are included on page 104 in the *Projects* section.

A BIT OF ADVICE

If you intend to buy a joint-maker, save up for one with a wide range of motion and interchangeable templates. Both simple and complex joint-makers are expensive, and the complex models don't cost that much more (relatively speaking) than their simpler cousins. Complex joint-makers and templates are available from:

Woodworker's Supply
5604 Alameda Place
Albuquerque, NM 87113

1-21 This joint maker lets you cut in all three dimensions. The worktable, which clamps the work in place, slides back and forth and side to side. You control both movements with a "joystick." The router can be moved up and down with another lever.

1-22 In addition to allowing a wide range of movement, this machine will follow *templates* — three-dimensional patterns for mortises and tenons, dovetails, and other fitted joints.

WHEN DO YOU NEED A SHAPER?

MUSCLE, STAMINA, AND VARIETY

If you can perform all of these woodworking tasks with a router, when would you ever need a shaper? The answer is that most home craftsmen don't. One or two portable routers, a router table, and a few other accessories provide all the routing *and* shaping capabilities most of us ever need. A shaper would be a waste of money and shop space.

However, there are times when only a shaper will do. Shapers remove more stock per pass and stand up to constant work better than routers. Also, there is a greater variety of molding shapes available in shaper cutters, and most of these cost less than large router bits.

SHAPER CHOICES

Although there are many different sizes and configurations, only two real categories of shapers are available — benchtop and freestanding. Most benchtop shapers are the crossbreed router/shapers mentioned earlier, while the larger floor models are true shapers.

FOR YOUR INFORMATION

One of the most important differences between routers and shapers is the type of motor. As mentioned previously, routers have universal motors, while shapers have induction motors. Induction motors generate much more torque. This is why a 1 horsepower shaper will work harder and longer than a 3 horsepower router! It's also why router/shapers don't qualify as true shapers.

Depending on the price you're willing to pay for a freestanding shaper, you can get many different features and capabilities. Here are a few things to consider when looking for one:

Fence — Just as the collet is the router's most critical part, the fence is the shaper's. There are many different fence designs and some are hard to live with. You should be able to adjust *both* halves of the fence independently — and make this adjustment easily and accurately. Also be certain that both halves remain *parallel* when you adjust them.

Stability — Any instability will interfere with the accuracy of the machine. Not only should the shaper sit solidly on the floor, but also the power train —

motor, pulleys, V-belt, quill, and spindle — should run without excessive vibration. (*SEE FIGURE 1-23.*)

Motor — Most shapers accept motors with between 1 and 5 horsepower. One horsepower is adequate for most jobs, but the machine may bog down when making heavy cuts — particularly if the cutter isn't as sharp as it could be. Opt for 1½ horsepower or more if it's available in the model you want. Remember that more powerful motors often require 220-volt electrical service. Also remember that more powerful machines should have beefier spindles. A ½-inch spindle won't stand up to the torque that a 2 or 3 horsepower motor can deliver.

A BIT OF ADVICE

The motors on most freestanding shapers have standard mounts and can be easily removed and replaced. If you can't get the power you need from the manufacturer, buy the machine without a motor, then purchase a motor from another source.

1-23 To check a shaper for excessive vibration, set a glass, full to the brim with water, on the worktable while the machine is running. If the water sloshes out of the glass or the glass walks off the worktable, something in the power train is out of balance.

Spindles — A machine with interchangeable spindles will give you the widest possible range of cutters to choose from. The two most popular sizes are ½ and ¾ inch in diameter, although a few of the largest machines accept up to 1½-inch spindles. If you're going to buy just one size, purchase a machine with a ¾-inch spindle. There are more cutters available in that size than any other.

Also consider the *spindle travel* — how far you can move the spindle up and down. Most freestanding machines offer about 3 inches of travel or more, but a few lightweight models move less than an inch. If you don't mind stacking bushings to move the cutters up and down the spindles, this may not bother you.

Worktable — The worktable should be large enough to safely support your work. The tables on some lightweight models are smaller than most router tables. Check that the spindle opening is large enough to accommodate your largest shaper cutter and that there is a ledge around the inside of the opening to support inserts. (*See Figure 1-24.*) This will let you use cutters of all sizes.

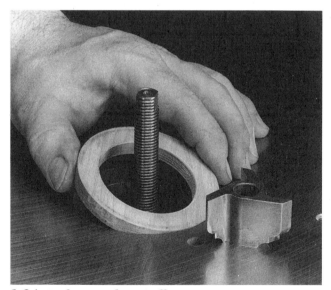

1-24   Make sure the spindle opening in your shaper is large enough to accommodate a large shaper cutter — or the largest cutter you ever expect to own. To use smaller cutters, make or purchase *inserts* for the opening. To properly support the stock as you feed it past the cutter, there should be as little space as possible between the inside edge of the insert and the outside edge of the cutter.

SELECTING BITS AND CUTTERS
IMPORTANT DIFFERENCES

Router bits and shaper cutters are similar in profile, and oftentimes the same shapes are available in each. There are, however, some important differences:

■ Router bits have shafts or shanks that fit in a collet. Shaper cutters have holes that fit over a spindle, allowing you to *stack* cutters on a spindle and combine shapes. (*See Figure 1-25.*)

■ You can make plunge cuts and piercing cuts with most *unpiloted* router bits, cutting downward with a hand-held router. (*See Figure 1-26.*) You cannot make these cuts on a shaper; shaper cutters only cut sideways.

TYPES OF BITS AND CUTTERS

There are an enormous number of bits and cutters, more than can be shown here. If you're new to woodworking, you may find the choice bewildering. But all these cutting accessories can be organized into four simple categories:

■ *Decorative,* used to cut molded shapes
■ *Joinery,* used to make woodworking joints
■ *Trimming/cutting,* used to cut or trim various materials
■ *Utility,* used for all three applications

"Common Bits and Cutters" on pages 22-23 shows examples of all four types of bits and cutters and their applications.

1-25   You can combine two or more molding shapes on a shaper by stacking cutters on the spindle. If you do so, take care that the cutting edges all face the same direction.

The most obvious difference between various bits and cutters is their profile. But there are other differences, too. You have the choice of a wide range of diameters among bits and cutters, even those with the same profile. Router bits vary from a 1/16-inch diameter to a 3 1/4-inch diameter, and shaper cutters may go up to a 5-inch diameter.

Some router bits — particularly straight bits — are available with different types of flutes for cutting various materials. (SEE FIGURE 1-27.) And in addition to single cutting accessories, there are also *universal* systems — a single hub or shaft which mounts knives and flutes of various shapes. (SEE FIGURE 1-28.) The universal shaper hub is sometimes called a "molding head," because of its resemblance to a table saw molding accessory. However, a true molding head's axis of rotation is horizontal, whereas a shaper's is vertical.

1-26 **One advantage of a shank-**mounted router bit over a spindle-mounted shaper cutter is that you can grind cutting edges on the end of the bit as well as on the sides. Most unpiloted router bits have either top-cut or point-cut flutes — flat or pointed cutting edges on the ends of the flutes as well as the sides. This feature lets you cut downward into the stock to make grooves, mortises, and other cuts in the *interior* of a workpiece. For example, a point-cut beading bit *(far right)* lets you cut quarter-round and half-round shapes in the surface of a workpiece, not just the arrises and corners.

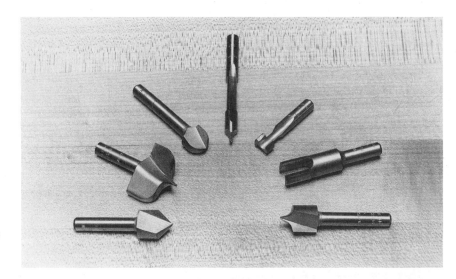

① ② ③ ④ ⑤

1-27 **Most router bits have** general-purpose *straight flutes* (1), designed for cutting both hardwood and softwood. Bits with *shear flutes* (2) leave a smoother cut and have an easier time plowing through hard, dense woods. *Spiral flutes* (3) help clear chips from mortises and interior cuts. *Stagger-tooth* (4) and *chip-breaker flutes* (5) are designed for cutting plywood, particleboard, and laminates.

1-28 **Universal** **cutting systems** consist of a single hub or shaft with interchangeable flutes or knives. The advantage of this accessory is that it saves money in the long run. Interchangeable knives are less expensive to purchase and to sharpen than single bits or cutters.

Finally, you have a choice of materials — what kind of steel the bit or cutter is made from:

■ *High speed steel (HSS)* — Because HSS is easy to machine, bits and cutters made from it are relatively inexpensive. It can be honed razor sharp, but it dulls

quickly. It's good for softwood (or occasional use in hardwood) but will not stand up to constant use in hardwoods. Some manufacturers coat the cutting edges of their HSS bits with a gold-colored titanium alloy to make them more durable. Titanium-coated HSS bits stay sharp longer than the uncoated variety, but they still won't hold up well in hardwoods.

■ *Tungsten carbide* — This is a much harder material than HSS and more difficult to machine, so carbide bits and cutters are expensive. To reduce expense, the flutes of most carbide cutting tools are just tipped or faced with tungsten carbide — the bulk of the tool is HSS. Carbide is brittle and can't be honed quite as sharp as HSS, but the cutting edge will last up to 15 times longer. (Some manufacturers coat their carbide bits with titanium not to improve durability, but to grind a sharper edge.) Carbide is a good choice

COMMON BITS AND CUTTERS

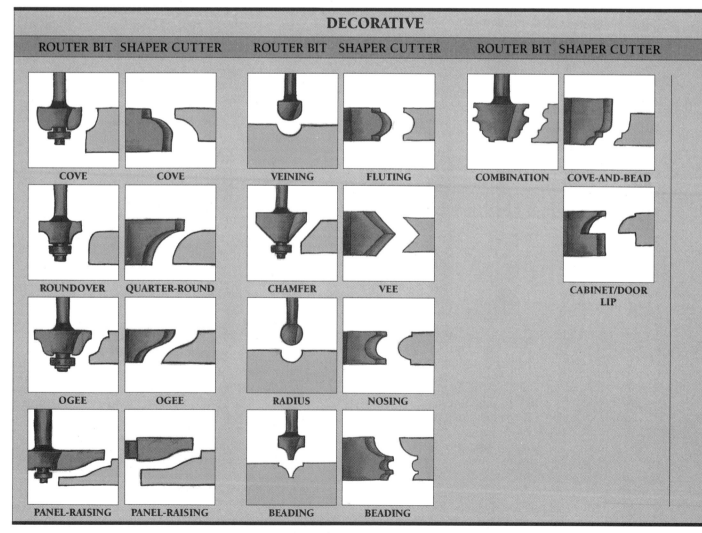

DECORATIVE					
ROUTER BIT	SHAPER CUTTER	ROUTER BIT	SHAPER CUTTER	ROUTER BIT	SHAPER CUTTER
COVE	COVE	VEINING	FLUTING	COMBINATION	COVE-AND-BEAD
ROUNDOVER	QUARTER-ROUND	CHAMFER	VEE		CABINET/DOOR LIP
OGEE	OGEE	RADIUS	NOSING		
PANEL-RAISING	PANEL-RAISING	BEADING	BEADING		

for bits that you use continually, or if you cut hardwoods often. Look for bits and cutters with thick, smooth-polished carbide cutting edges.

■ *Tangtung* — This is a relatively new material that stays sharp as long as carbide but will take an edge almost as well as HSS. Although it's not yet commonly available, tangtung is being used more and more. It's good for cutting both softwood and hardwood, but dulls quickly in plywood, particleboard, and other materials containing glues or resins.

A Bit of Advice

Put as much care and consideration into choosing bits and cutters as you would the machines that run them. After all, it's not the routers or shapers that do the actual cutting. A mediocre router outfitted with a good bit will cut a lot better than the world's greatest router with a mediocre bit.

Where to Find it

Don't see the cutter or bit you need in the chart? Or anywhere in your woodworking supply catalogs? You can have *custom* router bits and shaper cutters made to your specifications. These are expensive, but if you use the cutting accessory continually, it could be worth the money. Write:

Freeborn Tool Company
P.O. Box 3403
Spokane, WA 99220

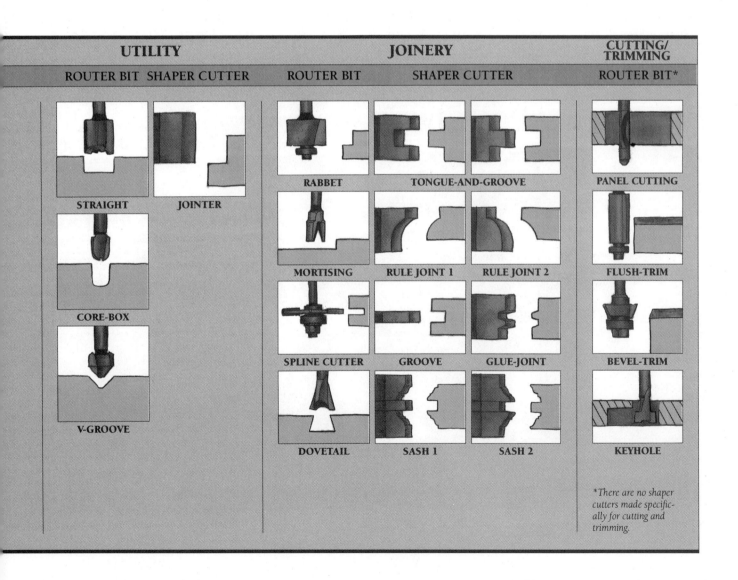

UTILITY

ROUTER BIT — STRAIGHT, CORE-BOX, V-GROOVE

SHAPER CUTTER — JOINTER

JOINERY

ROUTER BIT — RABBET, MORTISING, SPLINE CUTTER, DOVETAIL

SHAPER CUTTER — TONGUE-AND-GROOVE, RULE JOINT 1, RULE JOINT 2, GROOVE, GLUE-JOINT, SASH 1, SASH 2

CUTTING/TRIMMING

ROUTER BIT* — PANEL CUTTING, FLUSH-TRIM, BEVEL-TRIM, KEYHOLE

*There are no shaper cutters made specifically for cutting and trimming.

2

BASIC ROUTING AND SHAPING TECHNIQUES

Routers and shapers are simple machines and are uncomplicated to use. Alignment, adjustment, maintenance, and technique are all straightforward. You don't have to be a practiced expert to use either machine with precision. Just take care and be patient.

However, it isn't quite as simple as turning on a machine and feeding the wood into the cutter. Any tool, no matter how simple, is designed to be used in a specific manner and within specific limits. There are a few basic routing and shaping principles that you must keep in mind as you work.

ROUTING TECHNIQUES

A UNIQUE CHOICE

Each time you use a router, you have a unique choice: Do you pass the work across the tool or the tool across the work? If you use a shaper, this choice is made for you. The tool is stationary and you must feed the work. But the router can be either portable or stationary, depending on whether or not you mount a tool in a jig.

Choose whichever seems easier and safer — generally, the easier the operation is to perform, the safer it will be. If the workpiece is small enough to handle comfortably, mount the router in a jig and feed the work past the bit. If the board is large and heavy, take advantage of the router's portability and move the tool over the board. (SEE FIGURES 2-1 AND 2-2.)

A SAFETY REMINDER

If a workpiece is very small, your hands may come too close to the router bit as you cut it. In this case, you have two choices: You can rout the work with a portable router, using a commercially available foam rubber "routing pad" to hold the work; or you can rout a portion of a larger workpiece and cut a small piece from it.

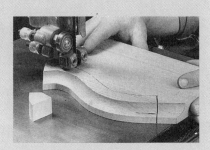

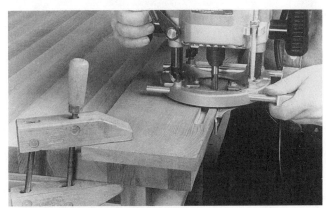

2-1 **Make sure that either the** workpiece or the router is stable and secure. They can't *both* move. If you choose to move the router across the work, clamp the work to your workbench. If a clamp interferes with the operation, rout up to it and turn the router off. Move the clamp to an area on the workpiece that you've already cut and resume routing.

2-2 **If you move the work across** the router, not only must the router be securely mounted in a jig, but also the jig itself must be secure. If the jig isn't heavy enough to stay put on its own, clamp it to a workbench or another stable fixture in your shop.

ALIGNMENT AND ADJUSTMENT

The first step in using any tool is to make sure that it's properly aligned and adjusted. There are only two things to check on a router. If you're using the machine as a portable tool, adjust the *depth of cut* (the distance the bit protrudes beneath the sole) and the *position of the guide* (if any). (*See Figures 2-3 and 2-4.*) If the router is mounted in a jig, adjust the *depth of cut* (the dis-tance the bit protrudes past the mounting plate) and the *position of the fence* (if any). (*See Figure 2-5.*)

Note: Remove only a small amount of stock with any one pass. (*See Figure 2-6.*) Set the depth of cut to take shallow bites, usually ¼ inch deep or less. There are few exceptions to this rule.

ROUTING RULES

Once you have adjusted your router, there are several rules of thumb you should review before turning on the machine. These apply whether you use the router as a portable tool or mounted in a jig:

■ Make sure the bit is properly mounted and the collet is secure. (*See Figures 2-7 and 2-8.*)

■ Make test cuts to check your routing setup. If an operation requires several different setups, make enough test pieces at each stage to carry you through the entire procedure.

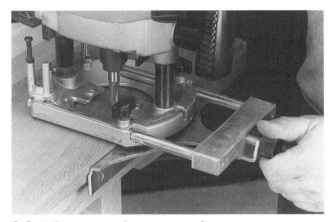

2-3 When using a base-mounted router guide (sometimes called a fence attachment), make coarse adjustments by sliding the two mounting rods in and out of the base. Make fine adjustments by turning the adjusting screw or knob. Remember to lock the guide to the rods before making a cut.

2-4 When using a straightedge to guide the router, position the straightedge perfectly parallel to your layout lines. Measure the distance between the straightedge and the layout lines at *several* places, not just the beginning and end of the cut.

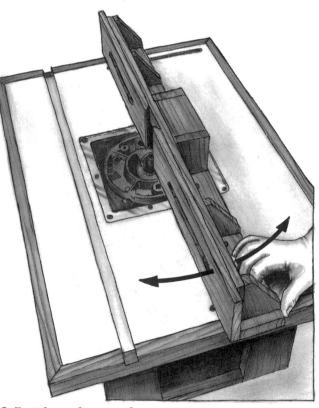

2-5 When adjusting the position of a router table fence, loosen the clamps at *both* ends of the fence and slide it forward or back. To make fine adjustments, tighten just *one* clamp and move the loose end of the fence.

■ Keep the router moving steadily as you cut. If you pause or move too slowly, friction will cause the bit to heat up and burn the wood.

■ Cut *against* the rotation of the bit whenever possible. If using a fence or straightedge, use the rotation to help keep the work (or the router) against it. (*See Figures 2-9 and 2-10.*)

■ Take note of the wood grain direction, and rout with the grain as much as possible to prevent the wood from tearing out. (*See Figure 2-11.*)

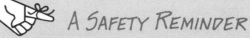

A Safety Reminder

Always wear both eye and ear protectors when routing. The need for eye protection is obvious — the router throws wood chips everywhere. The need for ear protection is less plain but just as necessary. A high-speed router motor generates high frequencies, which damage your hearing a tiny amount with each exposure. You won't notice a loss after just one routing session, but over time your hearing will grow less acute.

2-6 Never "hog" the cut when using a router — the tool is designed to remove only small amounts of stock at any one time. If you need to make a deep cut, rout your workpiece in several passes, cutting just ⅛ to ¼ inch deeper with each pass. (Generally, the harder the wood, the less you should remove with any one pass.)

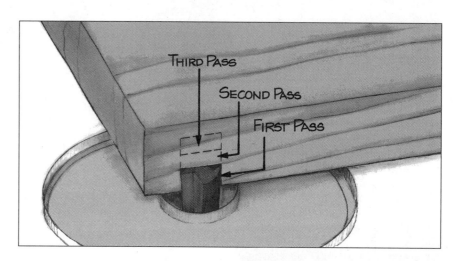

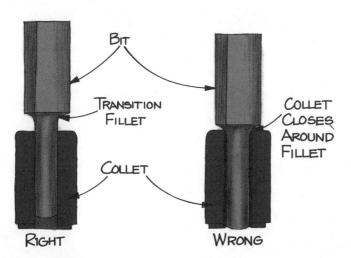

2-7 The shank of the bit must be inserted far enough into the collet for the collet to get a solid grip. If possible, the entire length of the collet should contact the shank. However, don't insert the bit so far that the collet closes around the *transi-*tion fillet — the portion of the bit where the shank ends and the flutes begin. If the bit is positioned incorrectly — inserted too far or not far enough — the collet may not grip the shank securely, and the bit may creep out of the collet when you rout.

2-8 To help position a bit properly in a collet, stretch a small rubber O-ring around the shank. This will prevent the bit from dropping down too far while you tighten the collet. **Note:** Leave the O-ring on the shank permanently — it won't interfere with the routing.

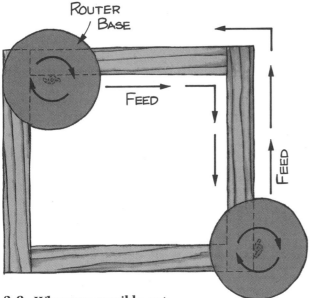

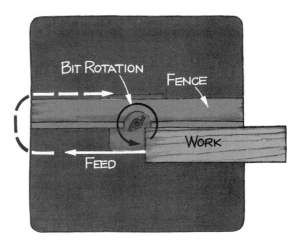

2-9 Whenever possible, cut *against* the rotation of the router bit — this will help control the router. If you rout with the rotation, the router (or the work) will try to pull itself out of your hands. How can you tell if you're routing against the rotation? Simple. Remember that the bit rotates *clockwise* when the router is used right-side up. To rout the *inside* of a piece, move the router *clockwise* around the perimeter. When routing the *outside,* move it *counterclockwise.* Treat fences and straightedges as if they were the outside of a workpiece — envision yourself cutting counterclockwise around these guides.

2-10 When the router is mounted upside down under a router table, the bit spins *counterclockwise* when viewed from above. Whether cutting the edge or the interior of a workpiece, imagine yourself feeding it *clockwise* around the fence — right to left as you face the fence. The rotation will help keep the board pressed against the fence.

2-11 Whenever possible, rout in the same direction as the wood grain. If you must cut across the grain, clamp a scrap to the edge of the board where the bit will exit. This will prevent splintering and tear-out.

HEIGHT GAUGE

It sometimes requires three hands to adjust the depth of cut on a router — one to raise or lower the motor, one to secure the height clamp, and one to hold the measuring device. If the router is mounted in a jig, you may also need a rubber back to scrunch down and read the rule.

This shop-made height gauge eliminates the need for one of the hands and most of the contortions. The gauge is stable enough that it doesn't have to be held, and the scale can be read accurately from most angles. Use the gauge with the arm facing down to measure heights of less than 3 inches and with the arm up for heights between 3 and 6 inches. This gauge can also be used with a shaper, table saw, dado cutter, or any tool or accessory in which the blade or cutter protrudes through a worktable or fence.

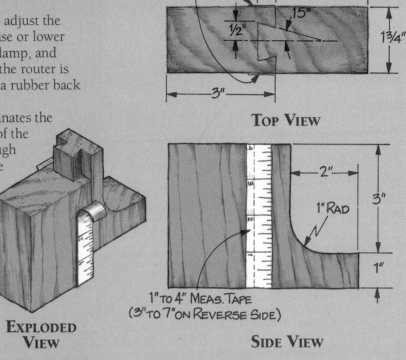

TOP VIEW

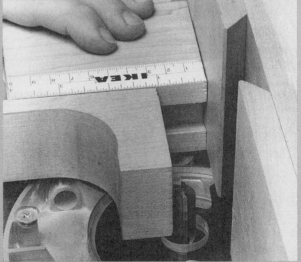

SIDE VIEW

1" TO 4" MEAS. TAPE
(3" TO 7" ON REVERSE SIDE)

EXPLODED VIEW

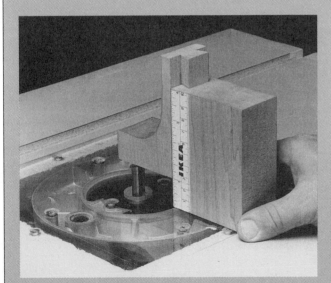

1 **To use the gauge, set it to the** desired height. Place it on the router sole or mounting plate with the arm over the bit. Raise or lower the bit until it touches the arm.

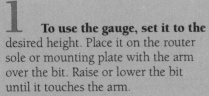

2 **You can also use the gauge to** measure the position of a router table fence in relation to the bit. Set the gauge and hold it against the fence with the arm encompassing the bit. Move the fence forward or back until the side of the bit touches the arm.

SPLIT ROUTING FENCE

Most router table fences have a single face. Both the infeed and outfeed portions of the fence remain in line; you cannot adjust them independently as on a shaper.

   However, there are some routing operations in which a split fence would be a boon — jointing, shaping an edge, cutting a joint in an edge, or any operation which removes stock from the entire edge. If you need such a fence, you can easily make one. This shop-made fence lets you adjust the positions of the infeed and outfeed faces separately, and the design can be adapted to fit most router tables.

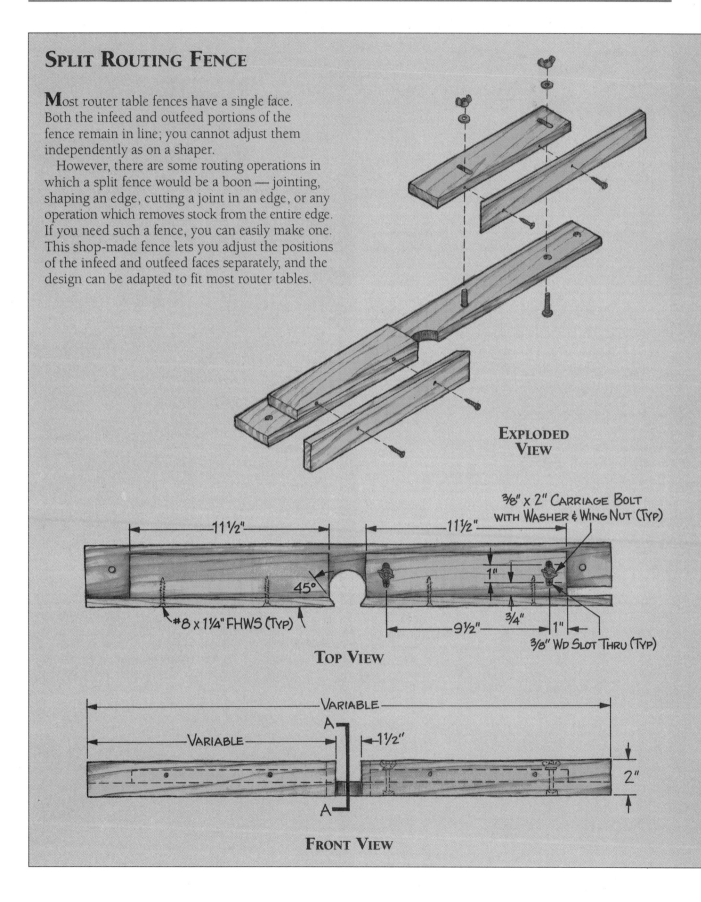

EXPLODED VIEW

⅜" x 2" CARRIAGE BOLT WITH WASHER & WING NUT (TYP)

11½"   11½"

45°   1"

#8 x 1¼" FHWS (TYP)   ¾"   1"

9½"   ⅜" WD SLOT THRU (TYP)

TOP VIEW

VARIABLE

A   1½"

VARIABLE   2"

A

FRONT VIEW

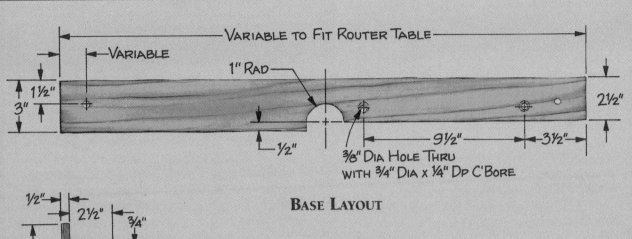

VARIABLE TO FIT ROUTER TABLE

VARIABLE

1½"

3"

1" RAD

½"

2½"

9½"   3½"

⅜" DIA HOLE THRU
WITH ¾" DIA x ¼" DP C'BORE

BASE LAYOUT

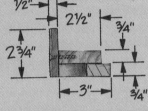

½"

2½"

¾"

2¾"

3"

¾"

¾"

SECTION A

1 **To adjust the split fence, first** position the *fixed* half of the fence in the same manner that you would an ordinary router table fence. Then loosen the *movable* half and slide it forward or back.

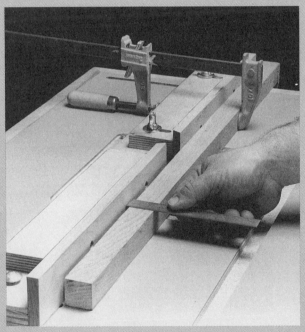

2 **The movable half of the fence** must be parallel to the fixed half. To check this, clamp a straight board to whichever half is farther forward. Measure the gap between the board and the other half — it must be the same all along the length of the fence half.

HAND-HELD ROUTING

In addition to the general rules discussed earlier, here are tips on *guiding* the router, whether you're using it hand-held or jig-mounted:

■ It's almost *never* a good idea to rout freehand (with the router unguided). The cuts won't be very accurate, and the router will try to pull itself all over the workpiece.

■ Always hold the router firmly with *both* hands. Be prepared for the initial jerk when you start it up — that annoying, momentary wrench can be difficult to control on some powerful routers. You may want to buy a router with a "soft start" motor to eliminate this unnerving tendency.

■ A router motor, like any spinning body, generates *centrifugal force.* Because of this, a router resists your effort to cut in a straight line. As you push it along, it will want to drift to one side or the other.

■ Make sure the router base is properly supported. When right-side up, routers are top-heavy. If the workpiece is too narrow, it may be hard to balance the router. (*See Figure 2-12.*)

TRY THIS TRICK

If you're routing a large mortise or removing stock from the interior of a board, the router will become increasingly difficult to balance as you cut away more and more of the supporting surface. To compensate for this, use the platform described in "Making and Using an Overhead Routing Jig" on page 16 as an oversized router sole. This will span the gap between the sides of the recess and keep the router from tipping.

USING PILOTED BITS

A piloted bit has either a ball bearing or a bushing to guide the cut. These pilots follow the surface of the work and keep the width of the cut consistent. Usually they are mounted to the ends of the flutes, but some are positioned between the shank and the flutes. (These are called "over-bearings.") Here are some tips for using piloted bits.

■ Remember that the pilot is meant to follow the contour of the board. When you set the depth of cut, the pilot must solidly contact the wood surface.

■ Anticipate the curves and corners to keep the pilot pressed firmly against the board's edge.

■ In trying to decide which way to move the router (or feed the work), treat the pilot as if it were a small straightedge or fence. With a hand-held router right-side up, cut *counterclockwise* around the outside of a workpiece. With the router mounted upside down in a router table, feed the work *clockwise* around the bit.

■ You'll need an extra guide when working on a router table — the pilot isn't enough. Use a *starting pin* to help control the work. (*See Figure 2-13.*) If you don't use a pin, the router bit could snatch the work out of your hands and fling it across the shop.

■ Remember that the diameter of the pilot controls the width of the cut. (*See Figure 2-14.*)

2-12 If you're routing the thin edge of a workpiece, or if the workpiece is too narrow to balance the router easily, clamp a wide scrap to the work to provide more support.

FOR BEST RESULTS

Use pilot *bearings* rather than bushings or pins. Bushings and pins turn at the same speed as the bit, rubbing the edge of the workpiece. Frequently, the friction causes them to heat up and burn the wood. Bearings turn independently of the bit, and don't rub or burn.

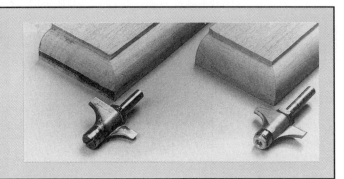

USING BASE-MOUNTED GUIDES

Base-mounted guides are available commercially as accessories for most standard and plunge routers. (You can also make your own by attaching a guide to an elongated router sole, such as the platform described in "Making and Using an Overhead Routing Jig" on page 16.) Like a pilot, the guide follows the edge of the wood. (*SEE FIGURES 2-15 AND 2-16.*) The technique for using it is similar to using a piloted bit, with one exception: Instead of holding both router handles, grasp one handle and the end of the guide. As you cut, keep the guide pressed firmly against the edge of the workpiece. Feed the router slowly and steadily.

USING GUIDE COLLARS

Guide collars attach to the base or sole of the router and follow a straight or contoured edge. However, as the name implies, these round guides *surround* the bit — the bit protrudes through them. Also, collars are rarely used to follow the edges of a workpiece. Instead, they are designed to follow *templates*. (*SEE FIGURE 2-17.*) When using guide collars:

■ Make sure that the bit does not rub the inside of the collar — that could ruin both the bit and the collar. (*SEE FIGURE 2-18.*)

■ Keep the collar pressed firmly against the edges of the template as you cut.

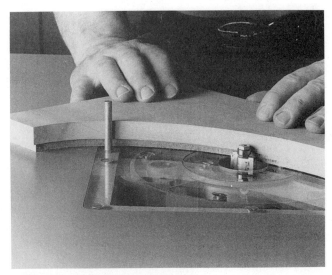

2-13 A *starting pin* provides a solid leverage point to help control the workpiece as you feed it into a piloted bit. Place the edge of the board against the starting pin, then gently pivot the wood into the spinning bit. Keep the wood firmly against *both* the pilot and the pin as you cut.

2-14 Adjust the width of cut on a piloted bit by changing the diameter of the pilot. Keep several different diameters on hand. **Note:** Not all piloted bits have interchangeable pilots.

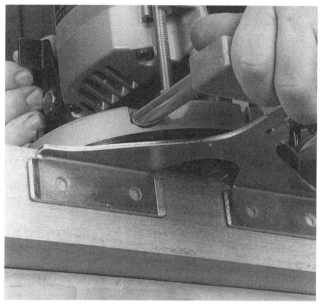

2-15 Most base-mounted guides will follow either straight or contoured edges, depending on the shape of the guide. Here, a straight guide — which looks like a small fence — rides along the straight edge of a board.

2-16 A round guide, such as this roller, will follow both convex and concave curves.

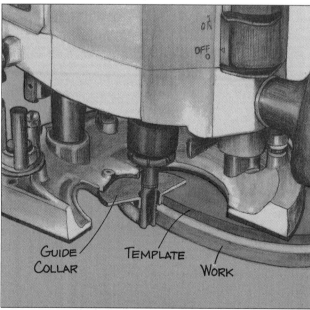

GUIDE
COLLAR   TEMPLATE

                                    WORK

2-17 Guide collars are designed to follow *templates*. As the collar traces the shape of the template, the bit cuts a similar shape in the workpiece. The routed shape may be a little larger or smaller than the template, depending on the relative diameters of the bit and the collar.

2-18 When using a guide collar, mount the collar first, then the bit. Make sure the bit is centered in the collar. If it's not, loosen the collar or the router sole (where the collar is mounted) and shift it slightly. Also make sure the flutes of the bit don't rub on the collar. If a collar is too small for the bit, use a larger collar — most collars come in sets of several different sizes.

USING A STRAIGHTEDGE OR A FENCE

The difference between a straightedge and a fence is all in how you hold the router. A straightedge guides a hand-held router over the workpiece; a fence guides the workpiece over a table-mounted router. Whether using a straightedge or a fence, keep whatever is moving pressed firmly against it. Feed the work or the router slowly and steadily — do *not* pause if you can help it. Here are a few more things to remember:

■ Make sure the straightedge or the fence is absolutely straight and flat; otherwise, your cuts won't be accurate. (*SEE FIGURE 2-19.*)

■ When using a fence, let it surround the unused portion of the bit. (*SEE FIGURE 2-20.*)

■ Always read the warp or bow in a board before you rout it, then keep the convex surface against the fence as you cut. (*SEE FIGURE 2-21.*)

2-19 To make sure a wooden straightedge or fence is straight and flat, run the guiding edge or face over a jointer. When jointing a router table fence, keep the base pressed flat against the jointer fence. This insures that, when mounted, the fence is square to the worktable. (The jointer must be properly adjusted, of course.) Make sure that any screws used to assemble the router table fence are recessed far enough that the jointer knives won't nick them.

2-20 When properly used, a fence not only guides the work but also protects you from the bit. Position the fence with only the cutting portion of the bit protruding in front of it. Unless you're routing a mortise or slot in the interior of a board, bury the unused portion of a router bit behind the fence.

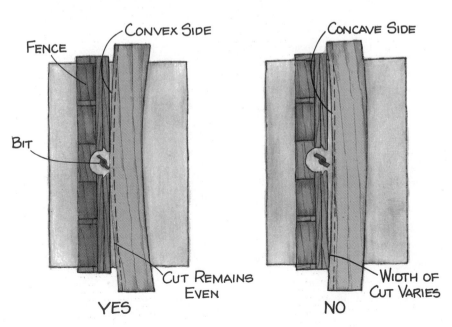

2-21 If your workpiece is warped or bowed — even slightly — keep the "proud" (convex) side of the bow against the fence as you cut. The width of the cut will remain the same from one end of the board to the other. If you turn the concave side toward the fence, the cut will be narrower toward the middle of the board than it will be at the two ends.

■ Whenever practical, use featherboards, push sticks, and push shoes to guide the work along a fence. (*SEE FIGURE 2-22.*)

2-22 When using a fence, attach featherboards to both the fence and the table to help keep the workpiece properly positioned as you feed it. Featherboards provide a firm, even pressure. They also prevent the workpiece from kicking back should it catch on the bit. Also use push sticks and push shoes to feed the workpiece — these keep your fingers out of danger.

USING A MITER GAUGE

Use a miter gauge on the router table to rout the end of a board or cut across the grain. Place the stock against the face of the gauge and feed it past the bit as if it were the blade on a table saw. There is an important difference, however. The rotation of a saw blade helps hold the work against the gauge; the rotation of the router bit pulls the wood sideways, making it "creep" across the gauge as you cut. There are several things you can do to prevent this:

■ Mount an extension — a long, auxiliary face — on the miter gauge, and clamp the work to this extension.

■ Clamp a stop to the miter gauge extension and butt the workpiece against the stop. (*SEE FIGURE 2-23.*)

■ Position a fence beside the miter gauge and let the end of the board ride along the fence as you cut. (*SEE FIGURE 2-24.*)

■ Tape 80- or 100-grit sandpaper to the miter gauge face with double-faced carpet tape.

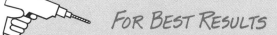

FOR BEST RESULTS

When using the miter gauge to rout across the wood grain, always back up the work with a scrap to prevent tear-out.

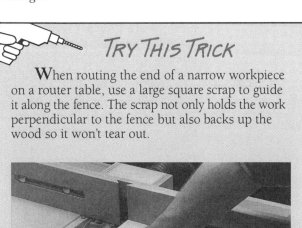

TRY THIS TRICK

When routing the end of a narrow workpiece on a router table, use a large square scrap to guide it along the fence. The scrap not only holds the work perpendicular to the fence but also backs up the wood so it won't tear out.

2-23 There are several things you can do to keep the work from creeping across the face of a miter gauge as you rout. Clamp the workpiece to a miter gauge extension, mount a piece of sandpaper to the extension, or butt the work against a stop.

PLUNGING AND MORTISING

Some operations require that you bore a hole with your router. For example, when you rout a mortise you must first make a starter hole with the bit, then enlarge the hole. This is easy to do with a plunge router — simply position the bit over the work, push down, and begin cutting. (*SEE FIGURES 2-25 AND 2-26.*) It's more difficult with a standard router; you must "rock" the bit into the workpiece before you can cut. (*SEE FIGURE 2-27.*)

2-24 You can also use a fence as a stop to prevent creep. However, the fence must be *precisely* parallel to the miter gauge slot. And you must be feeding the workpiece so the rotation of the bit pulls it against the fence.

2-25 To rout a mortise with a plunge router, clamp a straightedge or guide to the workpiece and adjust the depth stop. (You may also use a base-mounted guide attached to the router.) Position the router over the work, holding the base against the straightedge (or the guide against the work). Release the height clamp and push the bit down into the wood.

2-26 The depth stop will halt the bit at the proper depth of cut. Secure the height clamp and rout the mortise, keeping the router against the guide.

2-27 To cut a mortise with a basic router, again fasten a guide to the workpiece (or attach a base-mounted guide to the router). Set the router bit to the proper depth. Hold the router against the guide (or the guide against the work) with the base tilted at a slight angle so the bit is above the stock. Turn the router on and — still holding the base against the guide — pivot the router down, rocking the bit into the wood. When the router sole is flat on the workpiece, cut the mortise.

You can also cut a mortise with a table-mounted router, but the procedure requires careful layout work. You must mark both the router table and the workpiece to know when to start and stop cutting. (*SEE FIGURES 2-28 THROUGH 2-31.*)

2-28 To cut a mortise with a table-mounted router, adjust the height of the bit and the position of the fence. Put a piece of tape on the worktable in front of the bit and, using a small square, make two marks on the tape that indicate the diameter of the bit.

2-29 Using a square again, transfer the layout lines that mark the beginning and end of the mortise to a face of the workpiece that will be *visible* when you cut.

2-30 Place the workpiece against the fence, holding the portion where you want to cut the mortise above the bit. Turn the router on and lower the workpiece onto the bit, boring a starter hole.

2-31 Feed the workpiece into the bit until the right-hand layout line on the stock lines up with the right-hand line on the router table. Feed the work in the opposite direction until the two left-hand marks line up. At this point, the mortise is the proper length. If the mortise is deep, repeat this procedure several times, removing a small amount of stock with each pass until the mortise reaches the desired depth. **Warning:** There are a few exceptions to the rules governing feed direction, and this procedure is one of them. To prevent kickback, hold the work very firmly against the fence and feed it very slowly when "back-routing" (feeding the wood into the rotation of the bit).

SPECIAL JIGS AND GUIDES

From time to time, you may need a special jig or guide to rout a particular workpiece. For example, many woodworkers use a router, a straight bit, and a circle-cutting jig to make perfect circles. If you need a small circle (12 inches in diameter or less), it's easiest to cut the circle on a router table. Make the L-shaped *Small-Circle-Cutting Jig* shown and mount it to the router table fence. Cut each small circle by spinning the workpiece around the pivot screw.

To make larger circles, it's easier to use a portable router. Make the *Large-Circle-Cutting Jig* and attach it to the router base. This jig is just an elongated router sole. To cut a large circle, drive a nail or screw into the workpiece to make a pivot. Drill a hole in the small end of the jig, place the hole over the pivot, then swing the router around the pivot.

FOR BEST RESULTS

When using either circle-cutting jig, drive the pivot nail or drill the pivot hole into the *bottom* or *inside* surface of the workpiece. You don't want the hole left by the pivot to show on the assembled project.

In addition to cutting circles, you may need special guides to hold very small, wide, or tall boards while you rout them. Cut small workpieces by fastening them to a push shoe — the same safety device you might ordinarily use to feed larger stock past a blade or cutter. To cut wide and tall workpieces, clamp them to a simple T-shaped jig.

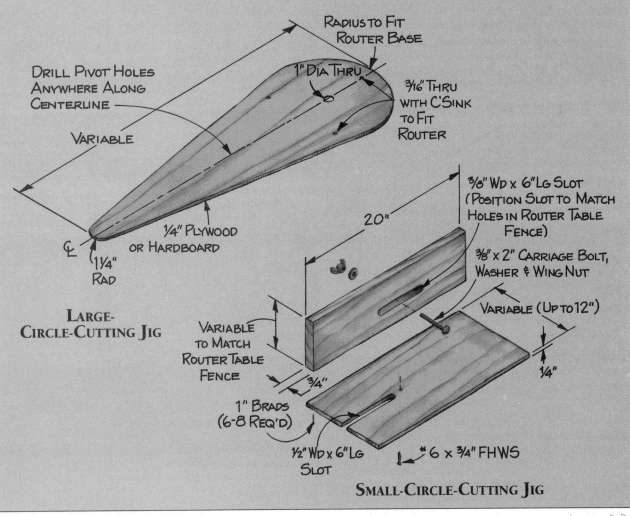

(continued) ▷

SPECIAL JIGS AND GUIDES — CONTINUED

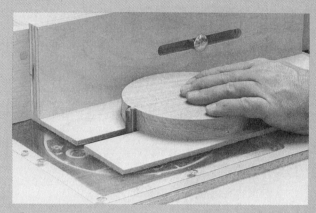

1   **Rout small circles on the** router table with this sliding work-table. Drill a small hole in the work-piece, the same size as the pivot screw. Adjust the diameter of the circle by moving the pivot closer to or farther away from the bit.

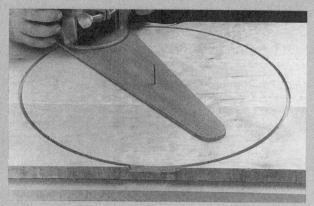

2   **Rout large circles with a** portable router and an elongated router sole. The distance from the pivot hole to the nearest edge of the router bit determines the diameter of the circle. **Note:** Put a scrap of ply-wood under the workpiece so the bit doesn't cut into your workbench.

3   **As mentioned, the safest way** to rout a small workpiece is to rout it while it is attached to a larger board, then saw it free. But on those occa-sions when this procedure won't work, stick the small piece to the bottom of a push shoe with double-faced carpet tape.

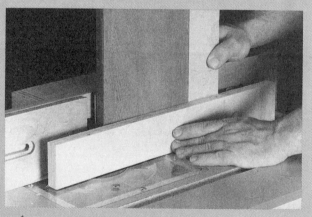

4   **To hold a wide workpiece** on edge against a fence, or to hold a long board on its end, parallel to the bit, use a T-shaped jig. Make this jig from scraps of wood or plywood. The long, vertical arm should be the same thickness as the workpiece. Note: *Glue* the arms together, don't screw them. Otherwise, you may nick a screw with the router bit.

ROUTER MAINTENANCE

Like most modern portable power tools, the router is a mostly maintenance-free machine. There are, however, a few things you must do to keep it in good condition:

■ Keep the motor free of dust. Use compressed air or a vacuum to clean out the housing regularly. Otherwise, the dust may work its way into the bearings — even permanently sealed bearings — and cause them to dry out and wear prematurely. *This is especially important if you use the router frequently on a router table.* When the router is upside down, the dust falls into the motor.

■ Keep the collet dust-free as well. Dust in a collet is the most common cause of bits slipping. If you don't keep it clean and the bits continue to slip, the collet will wear prematurely.

■ Replace the collet immediately if it shows signs of wear. A worn collet eats up the shanks of router bits. This may eventually ruin the motor shaft, requiring you to replace the entire armature.

■ Wax *and* buff the sole and the surfaces of the machine that slide together (such as the motor housing and the inside of the base). This will help these parts move freely and keep the router gliding smoothly across the work.

FOR YOUR INFORMATION

There is a common misconception that if you wax a woodworking tool, the wax will rub off onto the wood and interfere with applying a finish. This is not true as long as you *buff* the wax after it dries. Once buffed, the layer of wax remaining on a tool is only a few molecules thick — enough to protect and lubricate the metal, but not enough to ruin a finish.

Clean and maintain the router bits, not only the machine itself. After all, these are the most important parts of your routing system. Here are some tips:

■ If the cutting edges seem dull, touch up the flutes on a whetstone. (*SEE FIGURES 2-32 THROUGH 2-34.*) If they're extremely dull, have them professionally sharpened.

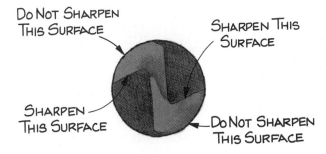

2-32 To touch up the cutting edges of a router bit, rub the cutting surfaces of the flutes back and forth a few times along the corner of a fine whetstone. Count the strokes, sharpening each flute an equal amount. This will keep the bit balanced.

2-33 Sharpen only the inside (flat) surfaces of the flutes. Leave the outside (curved) surfaces alone. If you try to sharpen these, you might change the diameter or the profile of the bit.

2-34 To touch up a carbide bit, use a diamond-impregnated sharpening stone. These are available from the same sources that sell whetstones.

■ After each use, remove dust and built-up pitch. (*SEE FIGURE 2-35.*) Then polish the shaft with a piece of steel wool or Scotch-Brite. (This polishing will not affect the diameter of the shaft — HSS and other tool materials are a lot harder than steel wool and Scotch-Brite.)

■ If there are any burrs or galling (rough spots) on the shaft, sand the shaft smooth with emery cloth. Carefully check the collet for dust or wear. Burrs and galling are a sure sign that the bit has slipped while you were cutting.

■ Lubricate pilot bushings and bearings every 1 to 2 hours of use. Wax and buff the bushings. Apply a *dry* lubricant, such as powdered graphite, to the bearings. Do *not* use oil or sprays such as WD-40. These will mix with sawdust, forming a gummy paste that can ruin a bearing.

SHAPING TECHNIQUES
ALIGNMENT AND ADJUSTMENT

Before you use a shaper, there are two adjustments to check. First, determine the *direction of rotation* of the spindle. (*SEE FIGURE 2-36.*) Second, adjust the *height of the cutter* above the worktable. (*SEE FIGURE 2-37.*)

SHAPING RULES

Many shaping techniques are the same as those for using a table-mounted router:

■ Make *test cuts* to check your setup before cutting good stock.

■ Always cut *against* the rotation of the cutter. (*SEE FIGURE 2-38.*)

■ Cut *with the grain* whenever possible; if you must cut across the grain, use a scrap to back up the wood and prevent tear-out.

■ To shape small parts, leave them attached to larger boards that can be easily controlled. After shaping, cut them free.

There are, however, a few important differences:

■ When shaping, use featherboards and push shoes to help feed the stock. *Push sticks are NOT recommended!* These sticks tend to catch on the cutter. A shaper can grab a push stick, whip it around, and fling it back at you like a spear.

■ For most shaping operations, you can remove all the stock in a single pass —there is no need to make multiple passes for deep cuts. The important exception to this rule is when using a 1/2-inch-diameter spindle. If you hog the cut, you can bend the slender spindle. You must also be careful when

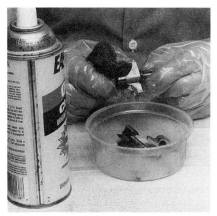

2-35 To remove the pitch from a router bit, soak it in lacquer thinner, or spray it with oven cleaner. Give the solvent a moment or two to work, then wipe off the bit with fine steel wool.

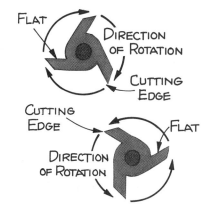

2-36 The shaper's direction of rotation is determined by how you mount the cutter. The spindle should turn in the same direction that the cutting faces — the *flat* surfaces on the cutter — are oriented. In general, it's best to run the spindle counterclockwise. The spinning motion tightens the nut against the cutter. **Note:** If you mount more than one cutter on the spindle, the cutting faces must all point in the same direction.

2-37 Most shaper spindles can be moved up and down 3 inches or more. However, a few travel only 1 inch or less. If this is the case, make a coarse height adjustment by stacking bushings or rub collars to position the cutter higher or lower on the spindle. (Keep the cutters as low as possible on the spindle. This minimizes the flex of the shaft, making for a truer cut.) Make a fine height adjustment by actually raising or lowering the spindle in the quill.

using a shaper/router. Because these tools have low-torque universal motors, you may have to make deep cuts in several steps.

■ To make a cut smoother, feed the work slowly so the machine makes more cuts per inch. You can't do this on a router; the tool spins so fast the wood may burn if you feed it too slowly. But burning is rarely a problem on a shaper unless you stop feeding completely.

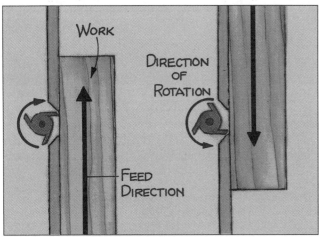

2-38 As on the router, you must feed stock over the shaper *against* the rotation of the cutter. Because the shaper motor is reversible, there is no rule of thumb for feed direction. You must pay careful attention to how you mount the cutter and which way it rotates. From this, determine how you will feed the stock.

SHAPING STRAIGHT SURFACES

Most of the operations you perform on a shaper will involve cutting straight, flat surfaces — usually the edges or ends of boards. When you shape a straight surface, you have three choices as to how to guide the work:

■ When shaping the edge of a long board or the end of a wide one, use the fence to guide the work. This involves some important adjustments. You must adjust not only the *overall* position of the fence, but also the *relative* position of each fence half and the *space* between the fence halves. Shapers have split fences for the same reason that jointers have split tables — most shaping operations reduce the width of the board as it passes by the cutter. You must adjust the infeed half of the fence to position the stock for the cut, and the outfeed half to support the stock after it's cut. You must also narrow the space between the fence halves as much as possible to support the stock near the cutter and prevent tear-out. The procedure for making these adjustments differs from shaper to shaper, depending on whether one or both of the fence halves is movable. (*SEE FIGURES 2-39 THROUGH 2-42.*)

■ To cut the end of a narrow board, use a miter gauge to guide the work past the cutter. (*SEE FIGURE 2-43.*) This requires less adjustment than a fence, but you must take some precautions to prevent the stock from slipping as you cut.

■ When working with short or narrow workpieces, use a sliding table. Some shapers come with these tables built in; on others, they're optional accessories. You can also build your own "Sliding Table Jig," shown on page 47.

2-39 When adjusting the position of a split fence with just *one movable face,* first change the position of the entire fence — both halves at once. Loosen the clamps and move the fence until the *fixed face* is where you want it.

2-40 Make a partial cut so you know how to adjust the relative position of the faces, then adjust the *movable face.* Loosen the clamp and turn the adjusting screw in the back of the fence. (If your shaper has two movable faces, simply adjust both faces independently.)

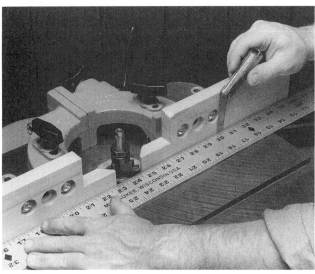

2-41 After adjusting the relative position, check that both fence halves are *parallel*. Hold a straightedge against the *forward* face and measure the gap all along the length of the back fence half — it should be even. **Note:** If the gap is too small to measure accurately with a rule, use an automotive feeler gauge. (*Cutter guard removed for clarity.*)

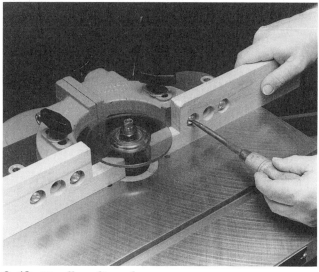

2-42 Finally, adjust the *space* between the fence halves and put the cutter guard in place. As on a router table, the fence should surround the unused portion of the cutter. In addition, the faces of most shaper fences slide left and right to narrow the gap between the fence halves. Not only is this safer, it also provides more support for the work as you feed it past the cutter.

2-43 When using a miter gauge to guide shaper work, the rules are the same as for a router table. Use a miter gauge extension for extra support, and clamp the work in place to prevent it from creeping. You can also use a stop to help position the work and hold it steady in the gauge.

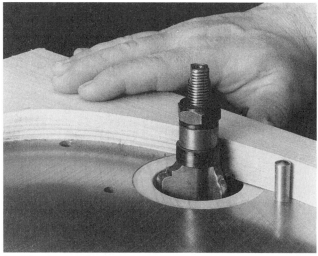

2-44 A *starting pin* provides a solid leverage point to help control the workpiece as you feed it into a collared shaper cutter. Place the edge of the board against the starting pin, then gently pivot the wood into the cutter. Keep the wood firmly against *both* the collar and the pin as you cut. (*Cutter guard removed for clarity.*)

SHAPING CONTOURED SURFACES

Shape curves or contoured surfaces by using rub collars to guide the work. These collars mount on the spindle with the cutter, and work like a pilot on a router bit. Many of the considerations for using them are the same:

■ As you cut, the rub collar must follow the shape of the board. Anticipate the curves and corners to keep the edge of the board pressed firmly against the collar.

■ Always mount a *starting pin* in the worktable when using rub collars. This will help control the work. (SEE FIGURE 2-44.)

■ The diameter of the rub collar controls the width of the cut. (SEE FIGURE 2-45.)

■ You can mount these collars above or below the cutter, as needed.

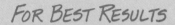

FOR BEST RESULTS

Use *ball bearing* rub collars rather than solid bushings. Bushings turn at the same speed as the cutter, rubbing the edge of the workpiece. They don't turn fast enough to burn the wood, as on a piloted router bit, but they may *burnish* it. This collapses the cell walls, making the surface hard and brittle. The workpiece may look fine after you shape it, but burnished wood won't accept a stain or finish evenly. Bearings turn independently of the cutter and won't burnish your work.

SHAPER MAINTENANCE

Because of its simplicity, the shaper needs less maintenance than most stationary power tools. Still, there are several maintenance chores that you must perform regularly to keep the machine running properly:

■ Keep the surfaces of the tool — particularly the work surface — free of sawdust. Every so often, vacuum or blow the dust out of the motor and the interior of the machine.

■ Keep the belts on belt-driven spindles properly tensioned. Replace worn or cracked belts.

■ Keep fence halves parallel. Non-parallel fences can cause uneven cuts or "snipes" at the end of cuts. If they are not parallel, readjust them so they are. On inexpensive shapers, there may be no way to adjust the fences to be parallel — either shim the old fences or make new wooden faces and joint them. (SEE FIGURES 2-46 AND 2-47.)

2-45 When shaping with a collared cutter, adjust the width of cut by changing the diameter of the collar. Most shaper spindles come with several different sizes of collars just for this purpose.

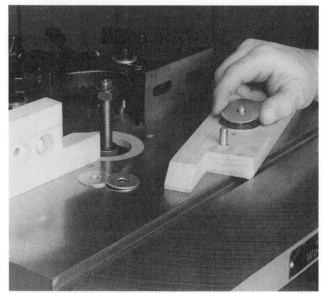

2-46 If the fence halves are not parallel, you can shim one face to bring it back into alignment with the other. Install metal shims — super-thin washers — on the appropriate fence mounting bolts, between the wooden face and the mount. Shim stock is available at most automotive supply stores. You can also use fender washers.

■ Check the spindle for run-out (a slight wobble). If the shaper makes a lot of noise when it cuts, or if the wood seems to chatter, the spindle may be bent, causing it to wobble as it turns. *(SEE FIGURE 2-48.)*

■ Wax *and* buff the fences and the work surface. The workpieces must glide easily across them.

In addition to maintaining the machine, also make sure the cutters are in good condition. Touch up the cutting edges when needed, and clean away the built-up pitch. *(SEE FIGURE 2-49.)*

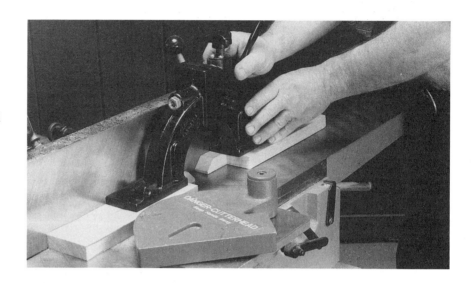

2-47 **Sometimes, the easiest and** best thing to do for a fence in need of alignment is make new wooden faces. Attach the faces to the fence and align them. Slide the fences together until there's only a small gap between them. Then joint both faces at once. **Warning:** Recess the bolts far enough into the wooden faces that the jointer knives won't nick them.

2-48 **To check a spindle for** run-out, remove the cutter, collar, and nuts. Hold a combination square next to the spindle and turn it by hand. The spindle should remain in contact with the edge of the square all along its length. If you see any daylight between the square and the spindle, you may have to replace the spindle.

2-49 **Shaper cutters can be** touched up in the same manner as router bits — rub the *flat* cutting surface back and forth over the corner of a fine whetstone. Count the strokes and sharpen each flute evenly to keep the cutter balanced. Don't try to sharpen the bevel surface; you could ruin the profile. **Note:** If this procedure doesn't restore the cutting edges after 15 or 20 strokes per flute, don't continue honing. Have the cutter professionally sharpened.

SLIDING TABLE JIG

A sliding table jig holds short and narrow workpieces *horizontally* to shape them safely. You can also use it to hold stock *vertically* when cutting tenons and surface grooves. It works equally well on both shapers and router tables.

The jig is just a souped-up miter gauge, and like a miter gauge it slides in the table slot. It has two worktables — one horizontal and one vertical. The two tables share a moveable quadrant (angle adjustor) with an adjustable clamp.

The parts of the jig can be reconfigured in many different ways, depending on the routing or shaping operation you want to perform. The vertical worktable can be mounted to the horizontal worktable, or removed from it. When mounted, the vertical worktable can move in or out in relation to the cutter. The quadrant can be mounted in four different positions — two on the horizontal worktable and two on the vertical. The clamp can be positioned on the quadrant as needed. Finally, the slide can be positioned to move the horizontal worktable relative to the cutter.

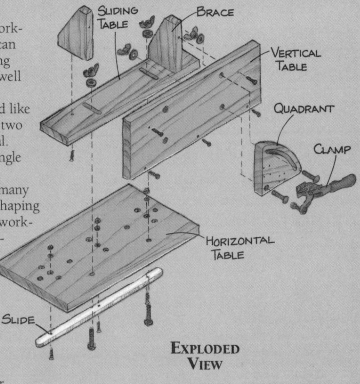

EXPLODED VIEW

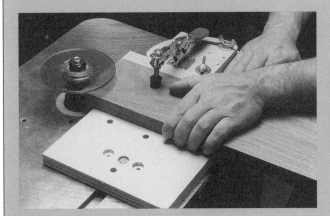

1 **To cut short or narrow stock,** rest the workpiece horizontally in the jig, against the quadrant. Clamp it in place. Place the jig in the miter gauge slot and slide it past the cutter. If needed, back up the stock with a scrap to prevent tear-out.

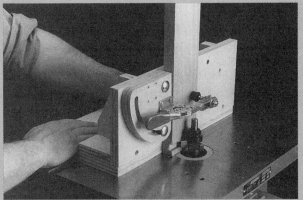

2 **To hold the workpiece** vertically, fasten the vertical table to the jig and move the quadrant to this table. Adjust the table to the proper distance from the cutter, making sure it's parallel to the miter gauge slot. Rest the workpiece against the quadrant, secure it with the clamp, and feed it past the cutter.

(continued) ▷

SLIDING TABLE JIG — CONTINUED

NOTE: Attach quadrants to worktable with ³⁄₈″ x 2″ carriage bolts, washers, and wing nuts. (2 Req'd)

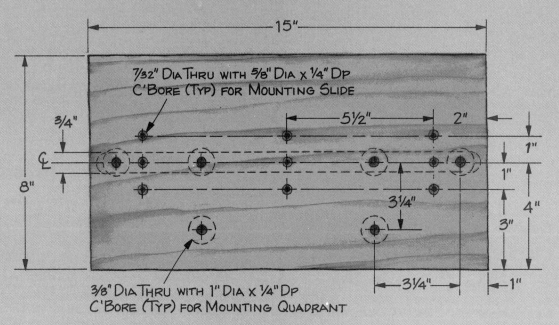

TOP VIEW

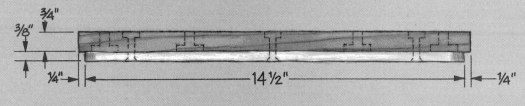

SIDE VIEW

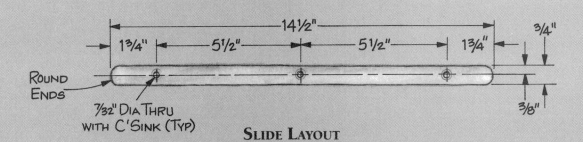

SLIDE LAYOUT

NOTE: Attach vertical worktable to horizontal worktable with ³⁄₈″ x 2″ carriage bolts, washers, and wing nuts. (2 Req'd)

HORIZONTAL WORKTABLE

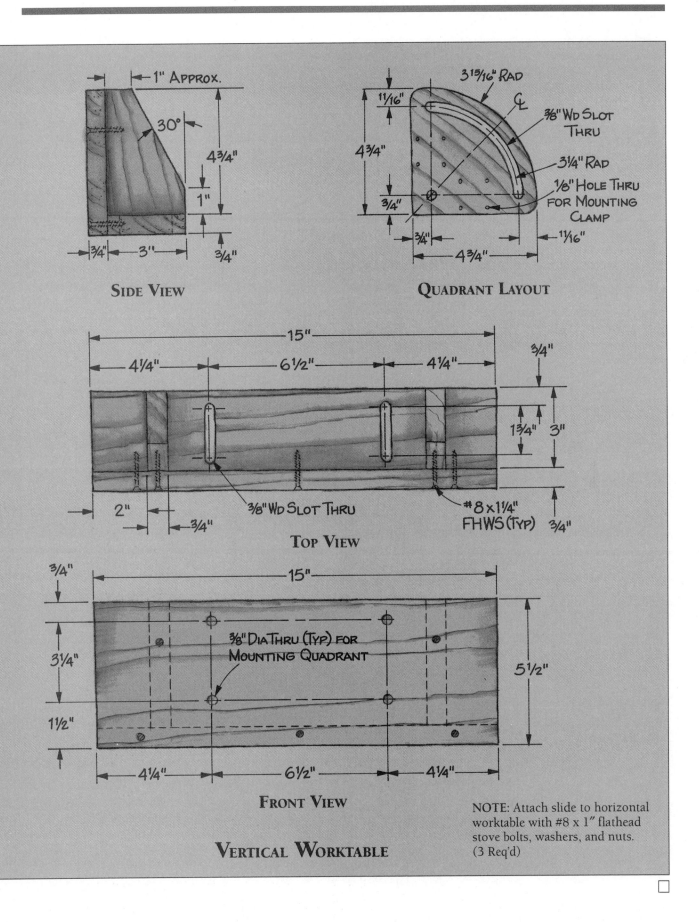

1" APPROX.

30°

4¾"

1"

¾" 3" ¾"

SIDE VIEW

3¹⁵/₁₆" RAD

¹¹/₁₆"

C̶L̶

⅜" WD SLOT THRU

3¼" RAD

4¾"

⅛" HOLE THRU FOR MOUNTING CLAMP

¾"

¾" 4¾" ¹¹/₁₆"

QUADRANT LAYOUT

15"

4¼" 6½" 4¼" ¾"

1¾" 3"

2" ¾"

⅜" WD SLOT THRU

#8 x 1¼" FHWS (TYP) ¾"

TOP VIEW

¾" 15"

3¼"

⅜" DIA THRU (TYP) FOR MOUNTING QUADRANT

5½"

1½"

4¼" 6½" 4¼"

FRONT VIEW

VERTICAL WORKTABLE

NOTE: Attach slide to horizontal worktable with #8 x 1″ flathead stove bolts, washers, and nuts. (3 Req'd)

3

ROUTER AND SHAPER JOINERY

Although routers and shapers were originally designed to create *molded shapes,* they can also be used to make *joints.* Routers, in particular, are excellent joinery tools — better in some ways than professional-quality mortisers and dado cutters. There are several reasons for this:

Simplicity — Setting up both hand-held and table-mounted routers is simple and straightforward. Shapers, too, are uncomplicated. Dedicated joint-making tools such as mortisers are more complex and require more time.

It's worth the effort to set up a mortiser if you're making dozens of duplicate joints. But if all you want to cut is a few mortises and tenons, a router or shaper will save you time.

Versatility — You can make a greater variety of joints with a router than with any other joinery tool. A shaper isn't quite as versatile, but you can still cut more types of joints on it than you can with a mortiser or dado cutter.

Accuracy — There is no more accurate joinery tool than a good-quality router or shaper. You may find tools that are just as accurate, but none more so. Furthermore, because these tools cut at a high speed, they leave a smooth surface. Smoothly cut joints fit better, and the glue bonds are stronger.

There are some disadvantages, of course. Most routers and home workshop shapers won't stand up to continual cutting as well as heavy-duty woodworking machinery. Because you cannot make deep cuts in a single pass on a router, it may take you longer to rout some joints than it would to use a mortiser or dado cutter. And, depending on the joint, you may be limited by the sizes and configurations of available bits and cutters.

These shortcomings, however, are minor. Routers and shapers are indispensable joinery tools in many workshops.

ROUTER JOINERY

JOINTING AND PLANING WITH A ROUTER

Before you can join two boards, you must prepare the stock by *surfacing* it — planing the faces and jointing the edges to make sure all the surfaces are straight and true. Routers are not the fastest surfacing tools — planers and jointers are usually more efficient — but you can prepare stock with a router if you need to. And there are times when a router will do a better surfacing job than either a planer or a jointer. For example, if you need to plane highly figured wood or surface a small board so it's very thin, a router with a wide straight bit may be the best tool. Routers won't tear out wild grain or chew up small, thin boards as planers do. However, to plane with a router you must make a special jig. (See "Router Planing Jig" on page 52.)

> ## FOR BEST RESULTS
>
> **I**f you do a lot of planing with your router, invest in a bottom cleaning bit, normally used to smooth the bottoms of mortises. It's available in diameters up to 1½ inches and cuts a wider swath than an ordinary straight bit.

You can also use a router and a straight bit to plane one surface flush with another. After applying a thin band of wood to the edge of a plywood panel, for example, rout the edging flush with the top and bottom faces of the plywood. Or, use it to cut screw plugs flush with the wood. Both of these operations require a special shop-made router sole. (*SEE FIGURES 3-1 THROUGH 3-3.*)

To joint the edge of a board, use a large straight bit and mount the router in a router table. Guide the board with the "Router Jointing Jig" on page 54. This shop-made straightedge has the outfeed face offset slightly from the infeed face. You can also use the "Split Routing Fence" on page 30 for this operation, if you wish.

3-1 To trim edging flush, make an oversized sole for your router with a ½-inch-thick block mounted to it, as shown. Adjust the height of the bit so it's even with the surface of the block.

3-2 Turn the router on and rest the block on the plywood with the bit over the edging. Push the router along the perimeter of the workpiece, cutting the edging flush with the plywood surface.

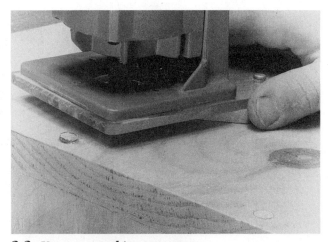

3-3 You can use this same setup to trim screw plugs flush with the surrounding surface. Just maneuver the bit over the plug.

ROUTER PLANING JIG

This jig enables you to plane boards up to 10 inches wide and 48 inches long to a uniform thickness, from 1½ inches thick down to about ¹⁄₁₆ inch thick. (If you need to plane larger or thicker boards, you can easily adjust the dimensions of the jig.) The router is mounted on the same platform used in "Making and Using an Overhead Routing Jig" on page 16. This platform rests on the sides of a shallow trough. Two stops, screwed to the underside of the platform, keep the router from cutting through the edges of the trough.

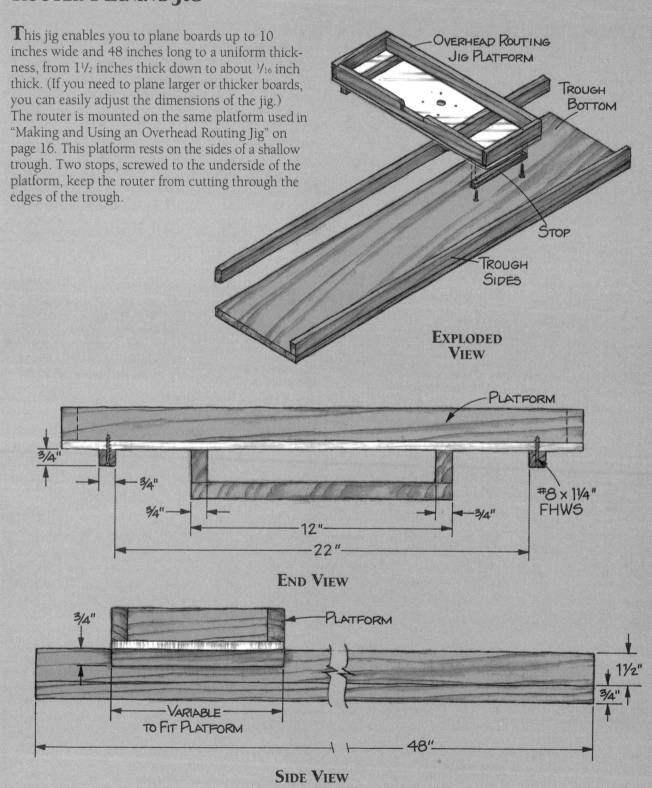

OVERHEAD ROUTING JIG PLATFORM

TROUGH BOTTOM

STOP

TROUGH SIDES

EXPLODED VIEW

PLATFORM

3/4"

3/4"

3/4"

12"

22"

3/4"

#8 x 1¼" FHWS

END VIEW

3/4"

PLATFORM

VARIABLE TO FIT PLATFORM

1½"

3/4"

48"

SIDE VIEW

1 **Since the router can only** remove a small amount of stock with one pass, you will save time if you *resaw* the wood on a band saw before planing it. Cut it to within 1/8 inch of the thickness you want.

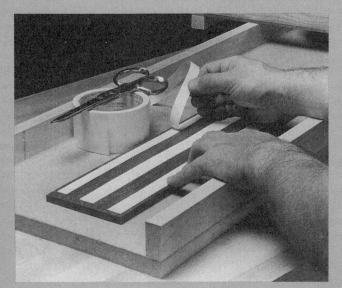

2 **Brush the sawdust from the** resawed board, then mount it in the bottom of the trough with double-faced carpet tape. If you don't trust the tape, screw the ends of the board to the trough. To avoid accidently nicking these screws, attach stop blocks to the edges of the trough, again using screws.

3 **With the board secured,** place the router over the trough and adjust the depth of cut to remove 1/32 to 1/16 inch of stock. Turn the router on and move it back and forth along the trough, planing the entire surface of the board. Repeat until the board reaches the desired thickness.

ROUTING RABBETS, DADOES, AND GROOVES

You can make the basic woodworking joints — rabbets, dadoes, and grooves — with a router and a set of straight bits. Which bit you use depends on the joint you want to make. If you're cutting a rabbet, choose the largest diameter bit available. If cutting a dado or a groove, use a bit that matches the width of the joint. To make a dado or a groove that's an odd size, choose a cutter that's slightly smaller than the joint and cut the joint in two or more passes. (*SEE FIGURES 3-4 AND 3-5.*)

3-4 When routing dadoes and grooves, the joint will ordinarily be the same width as the bit. Should you need to make a joint of an odd size, first make a cut that's somewhat *narrower* than the joint needed…

3-5 …then move the fence or straightedge to make a second cut, enlarging the joint to the desired width.

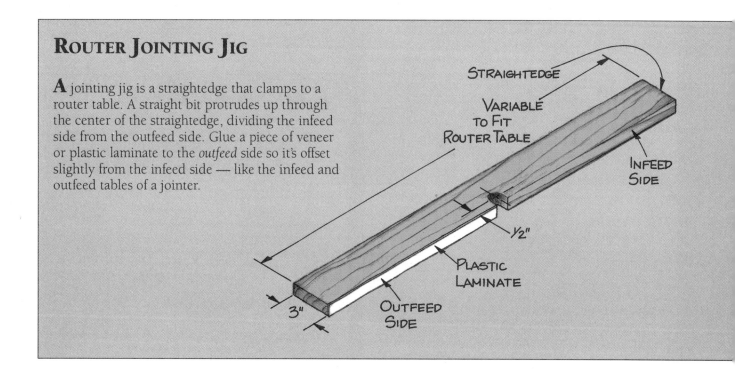

ROUTER JOINTING JIG

A jointing jig is a straightedge that clamps to a router table. A straight bit protrudes up through the center of the straightedge, dividing the infeed side from the outfeed side. Glue a piece of veneer or plastic laminate to the *outfeed* side so it's offset slightly from the infeed side — like the infeed and outfeed tables of a jointer.

STRAIGHTEDGE

VARIABLE TO FIT ROUTER TABLE

INFEED SIDE

½"

PLASTIC LAMINATE

OUTFEED SIDE

3"

TRY THIS TRICK

Make a rectangular router sole to help cut odd-sized dadoes and grooves. Cut the first side of this sole so it's the same distance from the axis of the bit as the radius of your regular sole. Make the second side $1/16$ inch farther away than the first one. Make the third side $1/8$ inch farther away, and the fourth, $3/16$ inch farther, as shown in the drawing. (You can also cut the sole so the sides progress in $1/32$-inch increments if you need more precision.) To rout an odd-sized joint — say, $5/8$ inch wide — mount a $1/2$-inch-diameter straight bit in your router. Make a pass with side one of the sole against a straightedge. Without moving the straight-edge, turn the router so side three is against the guide,

and make another pass. The sole will shift the router over $1/8$ inch to enlarge the $1/2$-inch-wide dado to $5/8$ inch.

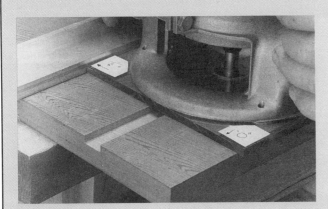

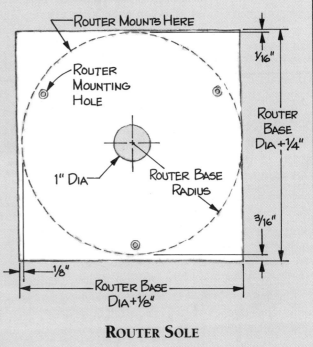

ROUTER SOLE

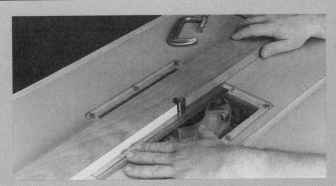

1 **Clamp the jig to the router** table with the infeed face to the right of the bit (as you face the jig). Adjust the height of the bit until it rises about $1/16$ inch above the top surface of the jig. Use a straightedge to position the jig so the outfeed face is tangent to the circumference of the bit.

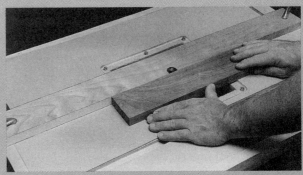

2 **Place the board against the** infeed face and feed it slowly from right to left. As the board passes to the outfeed face, the bit will remove a small amount of stock equal to the thickness of the laminate or veneer.

Since most basic joints are cut parallel to or perpendicular to straight edges, you must guide the router or the work in a straight line. Use an edge guide, straightedge, fence, or miter gauge. You may also wish to use a shop-made jig to help make the joint, such as the "T-Square Router Guide" on page 58.

If the joint is blind at one or both ends, cut them using the method described on page 38 or, attach stops to the workpiece or the guides to automatically halt the cut. (*See Figure 3-6.*) The location of these stops depends on where the joint is to be cut in the board. For example, to cut a blind groove that stops 6 inches from the ends of the board, clamp a stop to the outfeed side of the fence, 6 inches from the router bit. If the joint is blind at both ends, figure the distance between the two stops (DBS) by adding the length (or width) of the board (BL) to the length of the joint (JL) and subtracting the router bit diameter (BD):

$$BL + JL - BD = DBS$$

For example, if you wish to cut a 4-inch-long double-blind groove in a 10-inch board with a $^3/_8$-inch straight bit, position the stops $13^5/_8$ inches apart $(10 + 4 - ^3/_8 = 13^5/_8)$.

What if the rabbet or groove must follow a contour? You have several choices. You can use a *piloted* bit to follow the edge, or an *unpiloted* straight bit with a guide collar. If you use a piloted rabbeting bit, the bit follows the edge of the wood. (*See Figure 3-7.*)

If you use a straight bit and a guide collar, you must make a template for the guide collar to follow while the bit cuts the wood. Because this collar is slightly larger than the bit, the contour cut by the router will not be the same size as the template. For *inside* curves and corners, the contour will be *smaller.* For *outside* curves and corners, it will be larger. There will always be a small space between the edge of the template and the nearest side of the cut. To figure the width of the space (SW), subtract the diameter of the bit (BD) from the outside diameter of the collar (CD) and divide by 2:

$$(CD - BD) \div 2 = SW$$

For example, if you cut a contoured groove with a $^5/_8$-inch collar and a $^1/_2$-inch-diameter bit, the distance between the template and the groove will be $^1/_{16}$ inch $(^5/_8 - ^1/_2) \div 2 = ^1/_{16})$. When you lay out the template, make it $^1/_{16}$ inch smaller or larger than the groove you want to cut. (*See Figure 3-8.*)

ROUTING MORTISES AND TENONS

To make a mortise and a matching tenon, you must combine several of the techniques we have already discussed. Although it may seem complex, a mortise-and-tenon joint is a combination of several basic joints. A mortise is a groove that's blind at both ends; a tenon is made by cutting two or more rabbets in the end of a board.

The trick to cutting precise mortises and tenons is to make these simple cuts in the proper order. Most experienced woodworkers agree that it's easiest to cut the mortises first, then fit the tenons to them.

(continued on page 60)

FOR BEST RESULTS

The bit does not always fall in the exact center of a round router sole. Because of this, if the router turns while you're guiding it along a straightedge, the cut will not be accurate. The accuracy may also be affected when you remove and replace a sole, since the sole may shift slightly. To avoid this inaccuracy, put a spot of paint on the edges of the sole *and* base, one above the other. Always keep these spots toward you and directly opposite the straightedge as you rout. Each time you reattach the sole to the router, align the two spots.

3-6 When cutting blind joints — rabbets, dadoes, and grooves that are closed at one or more ends — use a stop block to halt the cut at the blind ends. Note that the end of the stop is mitered. This prevents sawdust from being trapped between it and the stock, where the dust might interfere with the accuracy of the cut.

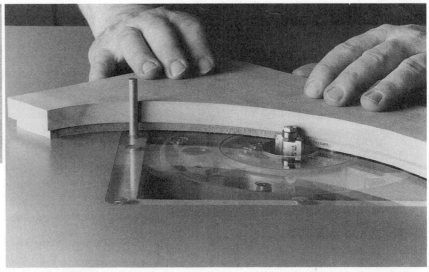

3-7 When cutting a joint in a contoured *edge,* use a *piloted* bit to follow the contour. A *piloted rabbeting bit* (inset, left) will cut an irregular rabbet, while a *spline cutter* (inset, right) will make a groove in an irregular edge.

3-8 To cut a curved or irregularly shaped groove in the *face* of a board, use a template and guide collar to guide the cut. Make the template from plywood or hardboard — the material must be slightly thicker than the height of the guide collar. Attach the template to the workpiece with double-faced carpet tape. Install the guide collar in the router and adjust the height of the straight bit to protrude through the collar. Rout the groove, keeping the collar pressed against the edge of the template.

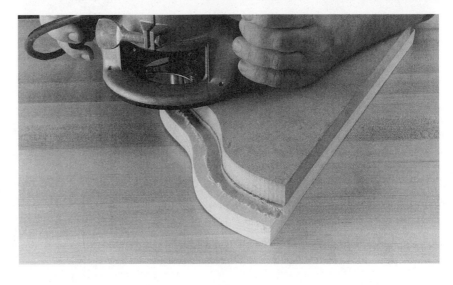

T-Square Router Guide

When using a hand-held router to cut dadoes, grooves, and rabbets, the most time-consuming part of the setup is positioning the edge guide or straightedge. This T-shaped jig simplifies this chore — use the short crossbar to instantly position the longer straightedge.

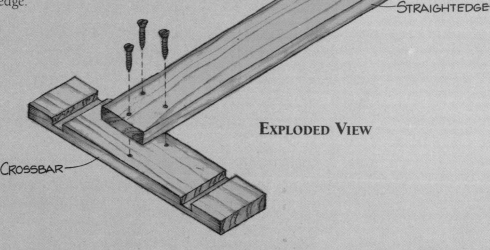

STRAIGHTEDGE

EXPLODED VIEW

CROSSBAR

1 **Before you can use this jig,** you must cut dadoes in the crossbar — one on either side of the straightedge. Place the jig over a large wooden scrap and butt the crossbar against an edge. Clamp the jig to the scrap. Cut the dadoes with a straight bit, keeping the router pressed against the straight-

edge. **Note:** Once you have cut these dadoes, you can only use the jig with that particular router and that bit — the dadoes won't line up properly with different tools. If you wish to use other routers or other bits, you must make additional jigs.

2 **Lay out the joints on the** workpiece. Place the jig across the wood, butt the crossbar against an edge or end, and line up one of the dadoes with the layout lines.

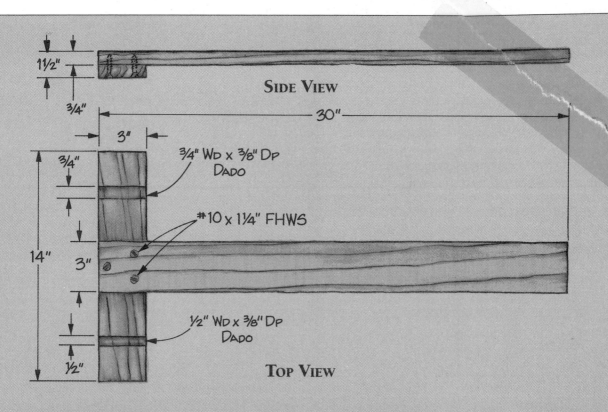

SIDE VIEW

1½"
3/4"
30"
3"
3/4" WD x 3/8" DP DADO
3/4"
#10 x 1¼" FHWS
14"
3"
3"
½" WD x 3/8" DP DADO
½"

TOP VIEW

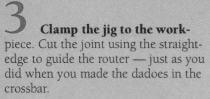

3 **Clamp the jig to the work-** piece. Cut the joint using the straight-edge to guide the router — just as you did when you made the dadoes in the crossbar.

4 **You can make a U-shaped** variation of this jig to cut joints that are wider than a particular bit. The arms of the U must be parallel to each other and perpendicular to the cross-bar. The distance between the arms determines the width of the joint.

To make a mortise, you must bore a starter hole and expand it to the dimensions needed, as explained on page 37. There are several ways to do this, using both standard and plunge routers, either hand-held or table-mounted. However, when you make mortises for mortise-and-tenon joints, you usually want to *duplicate* these mortises — make several of them in several different workpieces, all precisely the same size and shape. The easiest way to accomplish this is with a simple *frame* or template. *(SEE FIGURES 3-9 AND 3-10.)* You can also use an adjustable mortising jig. (See "Router Mortising Jig" on page 64.)

To calculate the *inside* length (FL) or width (FW) of a mortising frame, simply subtract the bit diameter (BD) from the diameter of the router base (RD), and add the length (ML) or width (MW) of the mortise:

$$RD - BD + ML = FL$$
$$RD - BD + MW = FW$$

For example, to rout a 2 x 2-inch mortise with a ³/₄-inch-diameter straight bit mounted in a 6-inch-diameter router, you must make a frame 7¹/₄ x 7¹/₄ inches on the inside (6 - ³/₄ + 2 = 7¹/₄).

The formula is similar for figuring the inside dimensions of a mortising template (TL and TW). Subtract the diameter of the bit (BD) from the outside diameter of the collar (CD) and add the length (ML) or width (MW) of the mortise:

$$CD - BD + ML = TL$$
$$CD - BD + MW = TW$$

After making all the mortises, cut the tenons to fit them. Using a table-mounted router, cut two or more rabbets in the ends of the mating boards. These rabbets will form the tenons. *(SEE FIGURE 3-11.)*

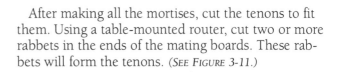
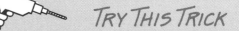

TRY THIS TRICK

In addition to routing square tenons, you can make round tenons with the aid of a V-jig. Clamp the jig to the router table, in line with a straight bit and perpendicular to the fence. Position the fence behind the bit to act as a stop. Feed a dowel or spindle along the jig and into the bit, turning it slowly. Stop when the wood contacts the fence.

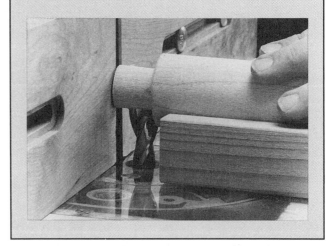

3-9 Use a simple frame to duplicate mortises in large workpieces. Position the frame over the workpiece, clamp it in place, and rout the mortise using the inside edges of the frame to guide the router. Later, you can square the corners of the mortise with a hand chisel, if necessary.

3-10 For smaller workpieces, you may want to use a guide collar and a template. Shown here is a commercial template for cutting hinge mortises. You can make your own templates by cutting the appropriate size and shape opening in hardboard or plywood.

3-11 To make a tenon, cut two or more rabbets in the end of a board — these rabbets will become the cheeks and shoulders of the tenon. To fit a tenon to a mortise, cut the tenon just a little large. Then slowly raise the bit, shaving away a paper-thin layer of stock on each cheek until you get the fit you're after. Guide the cuts with the miter gauge, using the fence as a stop.

ROUTING DOVETAILS

There are three common types of dovetail joints: half-blind dovetails, through dovetails, and sliding dovetails. (SEE FIGURE 3-12.) The router is the only power tool that can create them all. Rout these joints with a *dovetail bit.* (SEE FIGURE 3-13.)

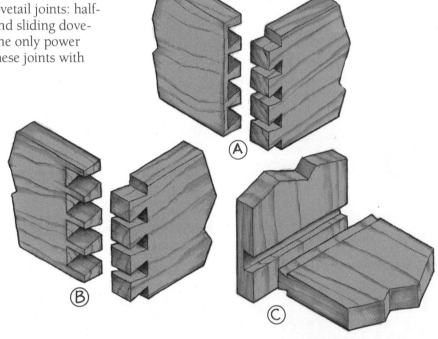

3-12 There are three basic types of routed dovetails. On *half-blind dovetails* (A), the joint is hidden from view on one side. This makes it ideal for drawers and other applications where you don't want to see the joinery. *Through dovetails* (B) are visible from both sides, and are often used for decoration as well as joining. *Sliding dovetails* (C) are sometimes called dovetail mortise-and-tenon joints. Like half-blind dovetails, they can easily be hidden.

3-13 Dovetail bits are available not only in different sizes, but also in different angles or *slopes.* Most bits have a slope between 7 and 12 degrees. **Note:** A few manufacturers make dovetail bits with slopes up to 15 degrees. These should be used for sliding dovetails *only.* Half-blind and through dovetails with slopes over 12 degrees may be weak — the sides of the tails become fragile and break off.

Both half-blind and through dovetails require special commercially manufactured templates. Half-blind dovetail templates are fairly inexpensive and easy to come by. They're also easy to use — you can cut both the tails and the pins of a joint in a single pass. (SEE FIGURES 3-14 AND 3-15.)

Through dovetails require two passes and two matched templates. (SEE FIGURES 3-16 THROUGH 3-18.) These templates aren't as easy to find as half-blind dovetail templates. And, because of the precision required to make them, through-dovetail templates are also more expensive.

3-14 To rout a half-blind dovetail joint, secure both of the adjoining boards in the template. The "tail" board is held vertically, so its end is flush with the top surface of the horizontal "pin" board. Cut both the tails and the pins in one pass with a dovetail bit, using a guide collar to follow the template.

3-15 The router cuts tails that are convex on one side. These fit concave slots between the pins.

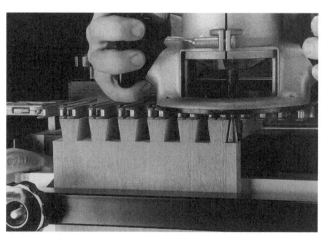

3-16 There are two types of through-dovetail templates available: fixed and adjustable. This one is adjustable — you can change the size and position of the tails and pins. Rout the tails first, using the tail template, a guide collar, and a dovetail bit.

3-17 Switch to the pin template and a straight bit to make the pins. Fit the pins to the tails by moving the template forward or back on its holder — toward the inside or the outside of the board. This will change the size (but not the location) of the pins.

Sliding dovetails require no special equipment other than a router and a dovetail bit. They are easier to make with a router table, although it isn't an absolute necessity. (*SEE FIGURES 3-19 THROUGH 3-21.*)

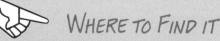

WHERE TO FIND IT

Through-dovetail templates are available through most mail-order woodworking suppliers, or you can write:

Leigh Industries
P.O. Box 357
Port Coquitlam, BC
Canada V3C 4K6

Keller & Co.
1327 I Street
Petaluma, CA 94952

3-18 Unlike routed half-blind dovetails, a routed through-dovetail joint has no convex or concave surfaces. A routed through dovetail looks just like a handmade joint. You can complete the illusion of handmade dovetails by scribing a few layout lines at the bases of the tails and pins.

3-19 To make a sliding dovetail, first rout a dovetail slot. Cut this slot the same way you would rout a dado or a groove. Because of the bit shape, however, you must cut the *full depth* in one pass. If you want to widen the slot, make additional passes, but don't change the depth of cut. Guide the board against the fence or with a miter gauge, as necessary.

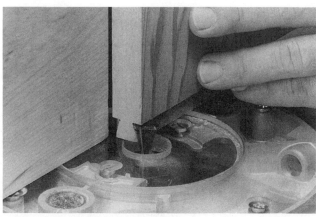

3-20 After routing the slot, cut a dovetail tenon to fit it. Leave the depth of cut unchanged, then pass a board by the bit, cutting one face. Turn the board around and cut the other face. The two cuts will form a tenon. **Note:** The tenon will be stronger if you make these cuts *across* the wood grain, as shown.

3-21 To assemble the joint, slide the tenon into the slot. The tenon should slide smoothly into the slot without binding. If necessary, adjust the fit by trimming a little stock off the cheeks of the tenon.

ROUTER MORTISING JIG

If you rout a lot of mortises of a particular size, it pays to make a rigid frame or template. Most woodworkers, however, cut many different sized mortises, depending on the project. You can use this *adjustable* frame with a standard router to cut any mortise up to 6 x 6 inches.

The frame consists of two interlocking L-shaped parts, glued up from strips of 1/8-inch plywood. The L-shapes slide together or apart. Two plywood tables hold small or narrow workpieces while you rout the mortises.

1   **To use the jig, first adjust the** frame to the required size. Calculate the inside dimensions of the frame using the formulas given in "Routing Mortises and Tenons" on page 60. Slide the parts closer together or farther apart as needed. Use a small square to check that the frame members are perpendicular to one another.

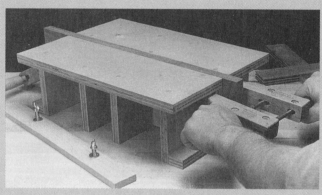

2   **If you wish to use the** plywood tables to hold the workpiece, adjust the ledges to support the workpiece. (For narrow pieces like the one shown here, you can support the piece with a single ledge.) Clamp the tables together with the work between them and the surfaces flush.

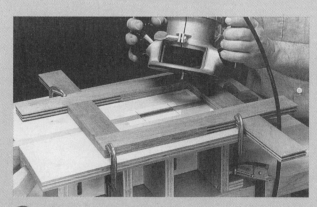

3   **Position the frame over the** workpiece. Clamp it to the tables (or the workpiece, if you're not using the tables). Rout the mortise, using the frame to guide the router.

4   **If you wish to duplicate** mortises with this jig, mark the surfaces with tape so you can accurately position the workpieces and the frame for each cut.

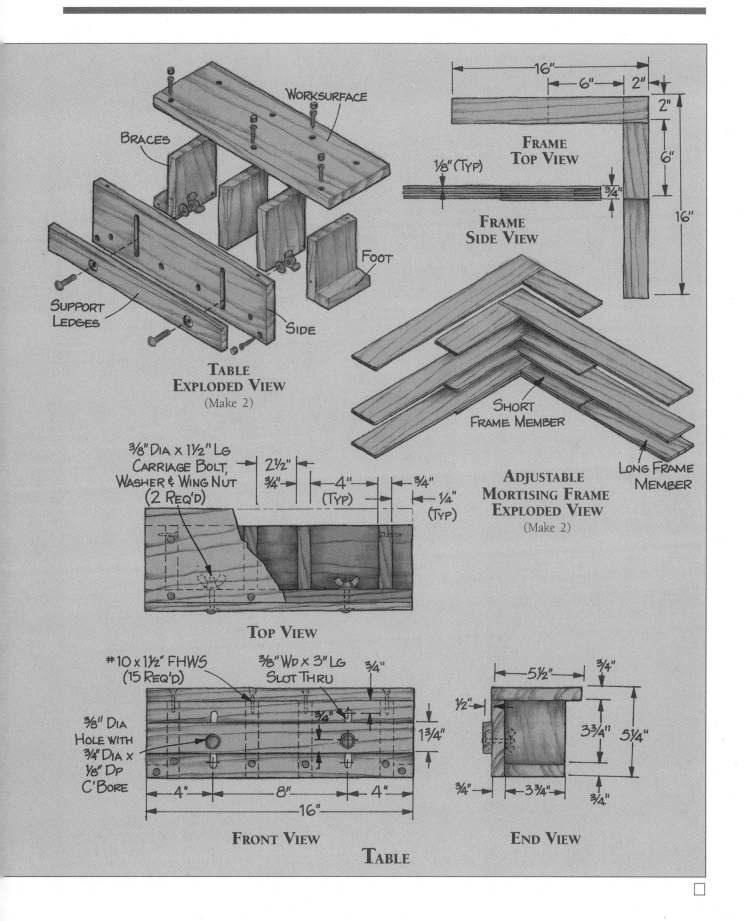

WORKSURFACE

BRACES

SUPPORT LEDGES

SIDE

FOOT

TABLE EXPLODED VIEW
(Make 2)

FRAME **TOP VIEW**

16"
6"
2"
2"
6"
16"
3/4"

1/8" (TYP)

FRAME **SIDE VIEW**

SHORT FRAME MEMBER

LONG FRAME MEMBER

ADJUSTABLE MORTISING FRAME EXPLODED VIEW
(Make 2)

3/8" DIA x 1 1/2" LG CARRIAGE BOLT, WASHER & WING NUT (2 REQ'D)

2 1/2"
3/4"
4" (TYP)
3/4"
1/4" (TYP)

TOP VIEW

#10 x 1 1/2" FHWS (15 REQ'D)

3/8" WD x 3" LG SLOT THRU

3/4"

3/8" DIA HOLE WITH 3/4" DIA x 1/8" DP C'BORE

3/4"
1 3/4"

4"
8"
4"
16"

FRONT VIEW

5 1/2"
3/4"
1/2"
3 3/4"
5 1/4"
3/4"
3 3/4"
3/4"

END VIEW

TABLE

DOVETAIL SPLINE JIG

The *dovetail spline* is a popular variation of the sliding dovetail. This joint is sometimes used to reinforce the mitered corners of boxes and chests. At first glance, it looks like a through-dovetail joint, but it's a dovetail-shaped spline that passes through the corner at 45 degrees.

To cut the slots for these splines, you must build the jig shown. This jig can be used with either a portable or a table-mounted router to cut both large and small boxes. If the box is large, clamp the jig to the corner of the box and use the straight-edge (shown in the drawings) to guide the router. If it's small, remove the straightedge. Clamp the box in the jig and rest the base of the jig on a router table. Use the router table fence to guide the jig (and the box) over the dovetail bit.

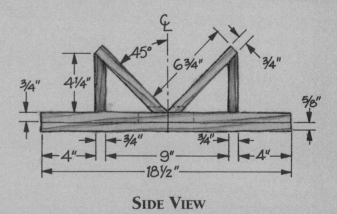

SIDE VIEW   FRONT VIEW

DOVETAIL SLOT

NOTE: Use router to cut dovetail slot. Dimensions of slot will vary with bit.

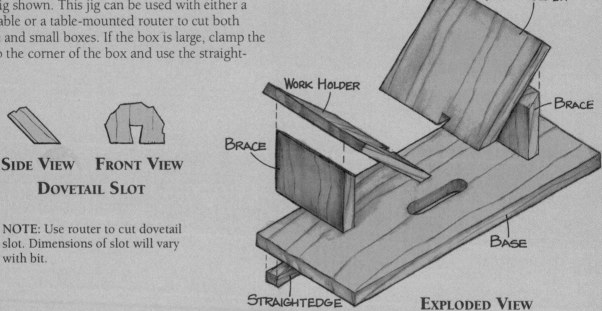

STRAIGHTEDGE   EXPLODED VIEW

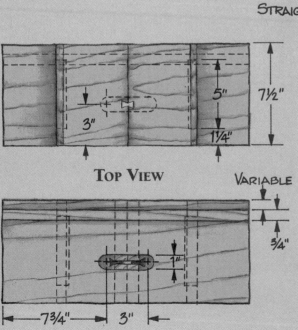

TOP VIEW

BOTTOM VIEW

SIDE VIEW

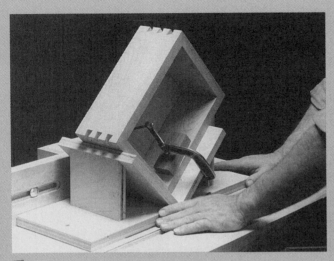

1 **When installing dovetail** splines in small boxes, position the jig on the router table with the dovetail bit protruding through the opening in the base. Adjust the fence to guide the jig. The base opening should travel back and forth over the bit. Clamp the box in the jig and cut a slot through one mitered corner. Loosen the clamps, slide the box forward or back in the jig, and cut another slot. Repeat, cutting several slots in each corner.

2 **If the box is very large, clamp** the jig to the box instead of the other way around. Fasten the straightedge to the base of the jig to guide the router. Rout a slot, move the jig, and rout another. Continue until you have cut all the slots needed.

3 **To make dovetail splines,** first cut a dovetail tenon to fit the dovetail slots in the corners of the box. Cut the tenon *with* the grain, along the edge of the board. Then rip the tenon free of the board with a band saw or table saw, making one long dovetail-shaped spline. Cut this long spline into short lengths.

4 **Glue the splines in the** dovetail slots. When the glue dries, cut and sand them flush with the surfaces of the box. **Note:** You can also use the surfacing sole shown in *Figures 3-1 through 3-3* to cut these splines flush.

SPECIAL ROUTER JOINERY

You can make all the joints we've discussed so far with just two bits — straight bits and dovetail bits. However, there are several router bits designed to cut specific joints in wood and other materials. I've already mentioned the spline cutter, which cuts a spline groove in or near a board's edge.

You can also use a spline cutter and a table-mounted router to cut lock joints — special tenon-and-dado joints for assembling drawer parts. *(SEE FIGURES 3-22 THROUGH 3-24.)* By making a special template, you can also use it to cut plate or "biscuit" joints, as shown in "Router Biscuit Joinery" on the facing page.

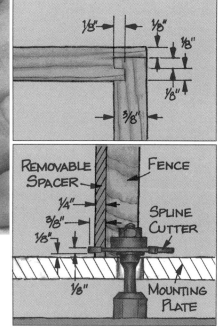

3-22   Lock joints often require three separate setups. Using a spline cutter and a spacer, however, you can make them with just one. First, cut a groove in the ends of the drawer front. **Note:** The inset shows how to set up to make lock joints in 3/8-inch-thick stock. By using different sizes of cutters and spacers, you can use this same technique with other thicknesses of stock.

3-23   Clamp the spacer to the fence. Hold the drawer front vertically against the spacer and cut the *inside* tenon short.

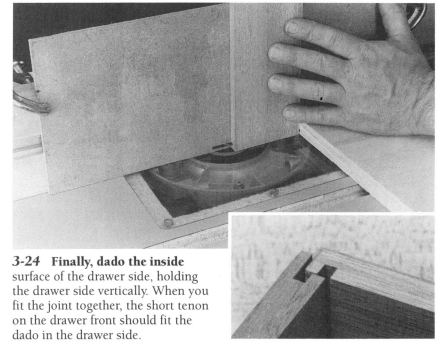

3-24   Finally, dado the inside surface of the drawer side, holding the drawer side vertically. When you fit the joint together, the short tenon on the drawer front should fit the dado in the drawer side.

ROUTER BISCUIT JOINERY

Among the various joints you can make with a router and a spline cutter are wooden plate or "biscuit" joints. Biscuits are small, football-shaped splines of compressed wood. They're used like splines and dowels to strengthen the glue bond between two boards. They come in several sizes — #0, #10, and #20 — for small, medium, and large joints.

Biscuits fit in oval-shaped grooves. To rout these grooves, first make a template, as shown in the drawings. The radius of the template shape will depend on the size biscuit you want to use, the radius of the cutter, and the radius of the pilot bearing. Assemble a $\frac{5}{32}$-inch spline cutter so the pilot bearing is between the shaft and the cutter. (The pilot bearings on most spline cutters are moveable.) Mount the cutter in the router.

Dry assemble the boards (*without* glue), mark them across the joint, then disassemble them. Align the mark on the template with a mark on one board. Clamp the template to the edge and rout a slot, following the contour of the template with the cutter's pilot bearing. Cut a matching slot in the other board.

To turn your router into a biscuit joiner, make a template with an oval-shaped cutout. Use the template with a piloted spline cutter to rout oval-shaped slots for wooden biscuits.

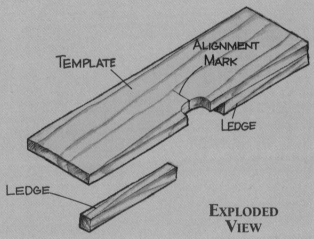

TEMPLATE

ALIGNMENT MARK

LEDGE

LEDGE

EXPLODED VIEW

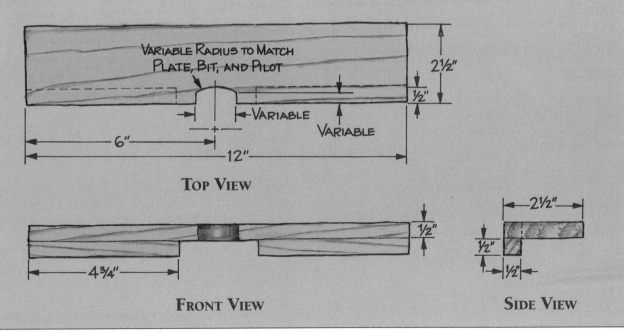

VARIABLE RADIUS TO MATCH PLATE, BIT, AND PILOT

2½"

½"

VARIABLE

VARIABLE

6"

12"

TOP VIEW

4¾"

½"

FRONT VIEW

2½"

½"

½"

SIDE VIEW

A T-slot cutter is another special joinery bit that makes a special keyhole-shaped slot for hanging plaques and picture frames. *(SEE FIGURE 3-25.)* A trim-mer bit joints veneers and plastic laminates as it cuts them to size. *(SEE FIGURE 3-26.)* There are others and manufacturers introduce new joinery bits all the time.

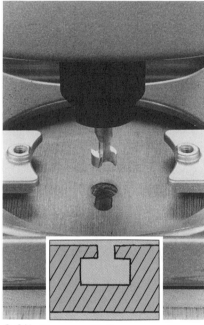

3-25 To use a T-slot cutter, it helps to have a plunge router. First, drill a hole with the bit, plunging it into the wood until the tops of the two small "wings" are slightly below the surface. Then move the router sideways, cutting a short, T-shaped slot.

3-26 A flush trimmer is a piloted straight bit — both the bit and the pilot are precisely the same diameter. This lets you trim an overlay of an veneeer or plastic laminate flush with the edges or ends of the under-layment. It also joints the edges of an overlay, allowing you to join another layer perpendicular to it. There are also bevel trimmers, which trim over-lays to size *and* leave a tiny chamfer. This chamfer "softens" the edge.

SHAPER JOINERY

MAKING JOINTS ON A SHAPER

You can make most basic joints on a shaper using jointer cutters and groove or slot cutters. *(SEE FIGURE 3-27.)* Cutting rabbets, dadoes, and grooves, however, is not the shaper's strong suit. The design of the tool limits not only the types of joints you can make but also their location. *(SEE FIGURE 3-28.)*

Despite its limitations, there are a few joinery opera-tions in which the shaper shines. With a jointer cut-ter, the shaper makes a good edge jointer. You don't have to make a special jointing jig, as you do with a router. Just set the right and left fence halves as you would the infeed and outfeed tables of a jointer.

The shaper is also a versatile tool for cutting grooves. You can even stack cutters to produce multiple grooves. *(SEE FIGURE 3-29.)*

3-27 The difference between groove cutters and jointer cutters is one of size, not design. Groove cut-ters are usually less than $1/2$ inch tall, while jointer cutters are at least 1 inch tall. Both have straight flutes.

3-28 The design of the shaper limits the basic joints you can cut with it. You must make rabbets and grooves in or near the edges and ends of boards. Dadoes are difficult, unless they're very near an end; joints requiring interior cuts, such as mortises, are impossible.

3-29 To cut several grooves in a workpiece in a single pass, stack groove cutters on a spindle. Space them apart with bushings or rub collars. *(Cutter guard removed for clarity.)*

MATED JOINTS

As a joinery tool, the shaper is most useful in making mated or *coped* joints — two shaped pieces of wood that interlock. Perhaps the most common example of coped surfaces is the drop-leaf or rule joint. This requires two mated cutters — a cove and a bead with precisely the same radii. *(See Figures 3-30 through 3-32.)*

A tongue-and-groove joint also requires two mated cutters. *(See Figure 3-33.)* A glue joint looks more complex than either of these joints, but it only requires one cutter. *(See Figure 3-34.)* A sash joint, on the other hand, may require as many as six cutters. *(See Figures 3-35 through 3-37.)*

3-30 A rule joint is not so much a joint as it is two decorative, mated edges between a tabletop and a drop leaf. Cut a bead and a fillet in the tabletop, and a matching step and cove in the drop leaf. *(Cutter guard removed for clarity.)*

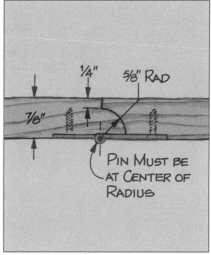

3-31 When the table is assembled, the bead will show when the leaf is down. When it's up, the joint will close and the surfaces will be flush.

3-32 The trick to making a rule joint is not as much in shaping the edges as in installing the drop leaf hinges. Each hinge must be mortised so that its pin is at the center of the arc described by the mating cove and bead. Fasten the long leaf of the hinge to the drop leaf, and the short leaf to the tabletop.

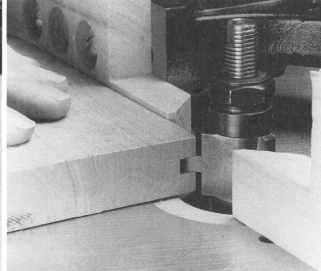

3-33 To make a tongue-and- groove joint, first joint the edges of the boards so they're perfectly straight. Cut a tongue in one edge. Then, without changing the height of the spindle, switch to the groove cutter and make a matching groove in the other board. (*Cutter guard removed for clarity.*)

3-34 To make an edge-to-edge glue joint on boards that are the same thickness, you don't have to change cutters at all. Just cut the two mating edges, flip one board over, and glue them together. You can also use a glue-joint cutter to join drawer parts at 90 degrees, but you must adjust the height of the cutter before you cut each adjoining board. (*Cutter guard removed for clarity.*)

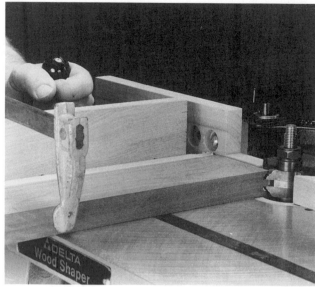

3-35 Sash joints are both decorative and structural. They are used to join the rails and stiles of door and window frames, and require between four and six cutters. There are two parts to each sash joint, the "coping" surfaces (the ends of the rails), and the "sticking" surfaces (the shaped edges of the rails and stiles). First, stack the coping cutters on the spindle and cut the ends of the rails. (*Cutter guard removed for clarity.*)

3-36 Remove the coping cutters from the spindle and stack the sticking cutters on it. Without changing the height of the spindle, cut the inside edges of *both* the stiles and the rails. (*Cutter guard removed for clarity.*)

3-37 Glue the rail ends to the stile edges. When assembled, the grooves and the decorative edges should run continuously around the inside of the frame.

4

EDGE AND SURFACE TREATMENTS

Both routers and shapers were developed to cut molded shapes in wood. Although their workshop role has expanded over the last century to include joinery and other operations, molding is still what they do best. They remain the chief woodworking tools for edge and surface "treatments" — cutting decorative shapes.

Using Decorative Shapes

A MOLDING PRIMER

Before we get into the techniques for making decorative molded shapes, let's review these shapes and how they're combined. In many woodworkers' minds, this is muddy water. No wonder — open any tool catalog to the router bit section, and you find whole pages of shapes, all in a jumble. However, there is some order to this chaos.

Despite the profusion of molding bits and cutters, there are really only three shapes in decorative woodworking — a bead (convex curve), a cove (concave curve), and a flat (straight line). Every molding, no matter how complex, is comprised of beads, coves, and flats. If you had only three router bits or shaper cutters — one for cutting beads, another for cutting coves, and a third for cutting flats — you still could produce any piece of molding, no matter how intricate the shape.

There's a little more to it, of course. Each of these categories is subdivided into a few basic molded shapes that can be cut with a common bit or cutter, as shown in "Basic Molded Shapes" below. All moldings are variations or combinations of these basic shapes. (*See Figure 4-1.*)

There are no hard and fast rules dictating how you combine these shapes or how you use them. However, you may find these guidelines useful:

■ Where the structural strength of a part is important, use simpler shapes. (*See Figure 4-2.*)

■ Consider where people will stand when viewing the shapes, and present these features at an angle that makes them easy to see and enjoy. (*See Figure 4-3.*)

■ Vary the shapes in a complex molding; don't repeat the same shapes over and over. (*See Figure 4-4.*)

Basic Molded Shapes

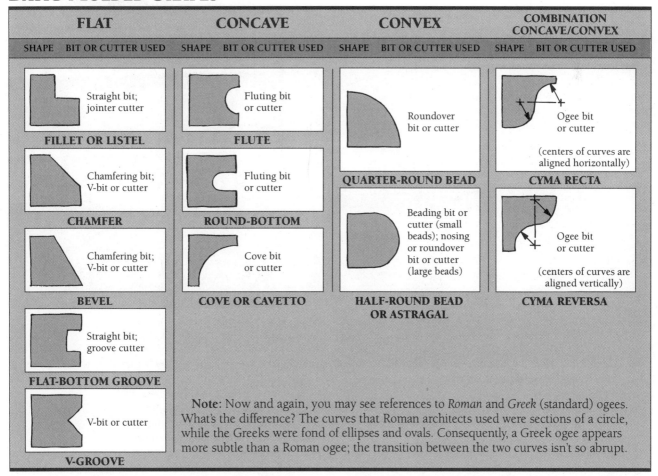

FLAT		CONCAVE		CONVEX		COMBINATION CONCAVE/CONVEX	
SHAPE	BIT OR CUTTER USED	SHAPE	BIT OR CUTTER USED	SHAPE	BIT OR CUTTER USED	SHAPE	BIT OR CUTTER USED
	Straight bit; jointer cutter		Fluting bit or cutter		Roundover bit or cutter		Ogee bit or cutter (centers of curves are aligned horizontally)
FILLET OR LISTEL		**FLUTE**		**QUARTER-ROUND BEAD**		**CYMA RECTA**	
	Chamfering bit; V-bit or cutter		Fluting bit or cutter		Beading bit or cutter (small beads); nosing or roundover bit or cutter (large beads)		Ogee bit or cutter (centers of curves are aligned vertically)
CHAMFER		**ROUND-BOTTOM**				**CYMA REVERSA**	
	Chamfering bit; V-bit or cutter		Cove bit or cutter					
BEVEL		**COVE OR CAVETTO**		**HALF-ROUND BEAD OR ASTRAGAL**			
	Straight bit; groove cutter						
FLAT-BOTTOM GROOVE							
	V-bit or cutter						
V-GROOVE							

Note: Now and again, you may see references to *Roman* and *Greek* (standard) ogees. What's the difference? The curves that Roman architects used were sections of a circle, while the Greeks were fond of ellipses and ovals. Consequently, a Greek ogee appears more subtle than a Roman ogee; the transition between the two curves isn't so abrupt.

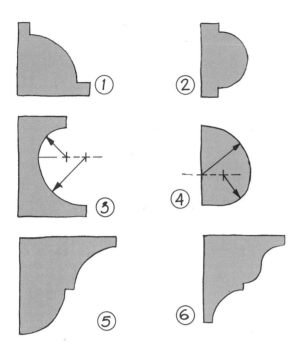

4-1 Complex moldings are
combinations of simpler shapes. The
ovolo (1) is a quarter-round bead
with fillets, and the *torus* (2) is a
half-round bead with fillets. The
scotia (3) combines two coves, each
a different size. The *thumbnail* (4)
combines two quarter-round beads.
The classic *bed molding* (5) consists
of a cove and a quarter-round bead
separated by a fillet. The *crown molding* (6) is a cyma recta (ogee) and a
cove separated by a fillet.

4-2 This tabletop will see a lot of
use, so the craftsman who made it
cut a thumbnail molding in the edge.
This relatively simple shape preserves
the strength of the edge. A more
complex shape would weaken it and
the edge would soon show the wear.

■ To make the moldings more dramatic, use sharp,
crisp transitions between the shapes. (*SEE FIGURE 4-5.*)

Once you have designed a molding, plan how you'll
make it — what bits or cutters you'll use, how many
passes will be required. Finally, consider how to incorporate the molded shapes in the project you're build-
ing. You have two choices: You can cut the shapes
into the surfaces of the structural parts, or you can
make separate shaped parts (moldings) and apply
them to the piece.

Each of these choices has trade-offs. If you make
applied moldings, you may not be able to match the
wood grain and color of the larger piece. But you can
use molding to disguise seams and joints. If you cut
the shapes in a large structural piece, you don't have
to worry about matching the wood. But you do have
to worry if the shape will weaken the piece. Choose
whichever molding design works best for the piece.

4-3 The molded shapes on this
antique corner cabinet are all angled
toward the viewer so they can be
seen easily. The shapes of the cornice
(top) molding face down, and those
of the plinth (base) molding face up.
The waist molding faces straight
ahead. Notice too that the plinth and
waist shapes have been kept simple,
since these will see more wear and
tear than the cornice.

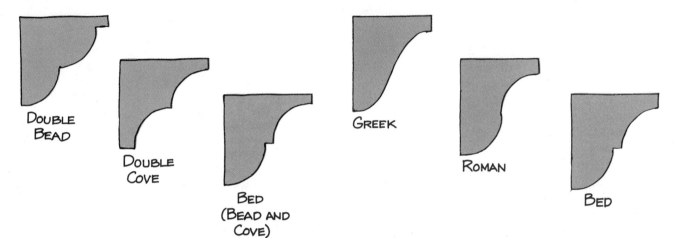

4-4 Vary the shapes to make the molding more visually interesting; don't repeat them too often. The classic bed molding, which incorporates a cove and a bead, has been a favorite of cabinetmakers and craftswomen for hundreds of years. You hardly ever see a molding with a double cove or a double bead.

4-5 For visual drama, the molded shapes should be distinct; the transition between them mustn't be nebulous. Make the curves and flats meet at distinct angles, or use fillets to separate shapes. For example, the Roman ogee (middle), is more dramatic than the subtle Greek ogee (left). The bed molding, in which the curves are separated by a fillet, is more dramatic than either the Greek or Roman ogees.

CUTTING DECORATIVE SHAPES WITH A ROUTER

EDGE TREATMENTS AND SIMPLE MOLDINGS

Craftsmen usually shape the *edges* of a piece. The reasons for this are both aesthetic and practical. Because the edges often trace the outline of the project, shaping the edges emphasizes and enhances the design. Also, the edges are easier to cut than the faces are.

The technique for routing molded edges is simple and straightforward; there's little here that hasn't been already explained. However, a few additional considerations are worth mentioning.

Before you rout a shape in a straight edge, make sure that the edge is as smooth and even as possible — joint it *and* remove the mill marks. If the edge is contoured, make sure all the curves are "fair" — smooth and even. (*SEE FIGURE 4-6.*) Since one of the purposes of a molded shape is to emphasize the edge, the shape will also emphasize any imperfections in the edge.

When you're ready to shape the piece, cut the ends (end grain) first, then the edges (long grain). (*SEE FIGURES 4-7 AND 4-8.*) Cut large parts with a hand-held

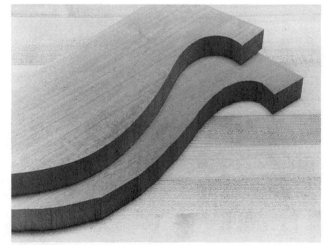

4-6 Before you rout a curved edge, make sure the curves are "fair" — the curves must seem smooth and flowing, with no inappropriate flats or abrupt changes of circumference. If the curve is a circle or an oval, the shape must be regular and symmetrical.

router, and small parts on a router table. Leave very small parts attached to a larger board, rout the edge of the board, then cut them free. This last technique is particularly important when making moldings. Most moldings, when ripped to their final dimensions, are too slender to rout safely. The cutting action of the router may tear the thin stock apart. *(See Figures 4-9 through 4-11.)*

If you use a large bit, such as a panel-raising bit, slow down the speed (rpm) of the router. *(See Figure 4-12.)* The larger the bit, the slower you should run the router — otherwise the bit may burn the wood. If you can't vary the speed of the router, you shouldn't use bits over 2 inches in diameter. Even bits over 1½ inches can be troublesome.

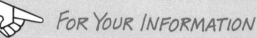

FOR YOUR INFORMATION

Manufacturers sometimes coat the cutting edges of large, carbide-tipped router bits with a gold-colored titanium alloy and claim the bits can be used safely without reducing the routing speed. This is true to a certain extent. Titanium-coated carbide can be honed to a much sharper edge than the uncoated variety. While the cutting edges remain razor sharp, the bit will cut cleanly at high speeds. But as soon as the edges dull or load up with pitch, the bit will burn the wood.

4-7 When you rout a shape around the perimeter of a board, cut the two *ends* first. The grain at the corners will probably tear slightly as you finish each cut, but don't worry…

4-8 … when you rout the edges, you'll remove any torn grain.

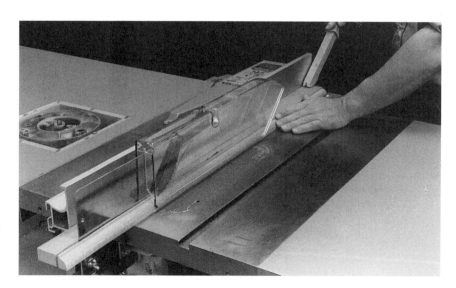

4-9 To make an applied molding or picture frame stock, cut the shape you want in the edge of a *wide* board, then rip it to the proper thickness on a table saw. Don't try to rout a shape in narrow stock; it may chip, splinter, or kick back.

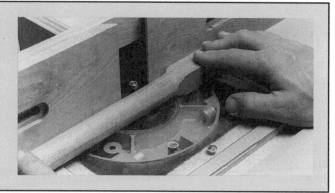

TRY THIS TRICK

By rounding-over the four *arrises* of a square workpiece (where the edges and faces meet), you can make your own dowels on a router table. This is especially useful if you need a dowel made from a particular species of wood. The width and thickness of the workpiece must be *precisely twice* the radius of the bit. As you rout, leave about 2 inches of stock uncut (square) on either end of the workpiece. This will keep the work stable on the router table.

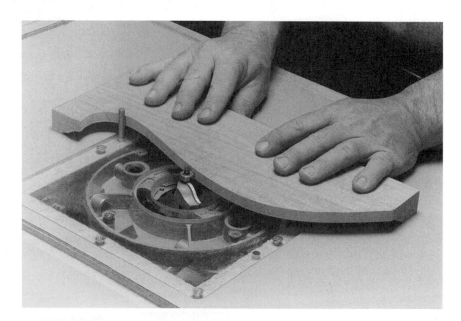

4-10 **This safety consideration** also applies to making curved moldings, such as a classic "gooseneck" molding. Cut the *inside* curve in the wide molding stock, sand it so the curves are fair, then rout the shape in the edge.

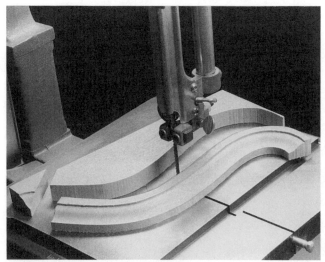

4-11 **When you have shaped the** inside edge, cut the outside edge to free the molding from the workpiece.

4-12 **When using large bits, such** as panel-raising bits, slow the rotation of the router. Cut the shape in several extra-light passes, removing just $1/16$ inch of stock at a time.

SURFACE TREATMENTS

In addition to cutting edges, you can create a variety of decorative shapes in the face of a workpiece. Surface treatments can be cut with either a hand-held or a table-mounted router fitted with an unpiloted or point-cut bit.

The most common surface decoration is a simple groove — flat-bottom, round-bottom, or V-bottom. If the groove is straight, use a straightedge, fence, or miter gauge to guide the cut. (*SEE FIGURE 4-13.*) If the groove is irregular, use a guide collar and a template. (*SEE FIGURE 4-14.*)

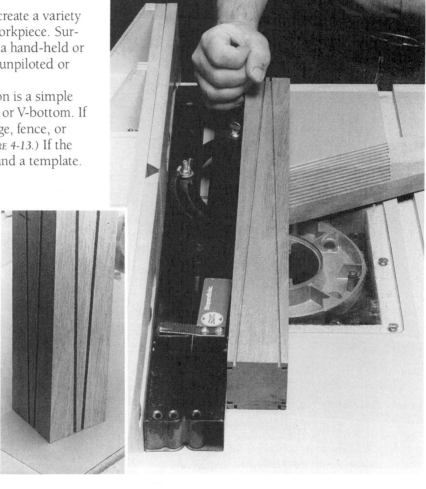

4-13 When cutting straight grooves, you can use a variety of jigs to get a decorative effect. Here, a tapering jig produces a pattern of angled grooves in a table leg. The grooves create the impression of a tapered leg, even though the leg is straight.

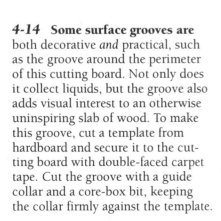

4-14 Some surface grooves are both decorative *and* practical, such as the groove around the perimeter of this cutting board. Not only does it collect liquids, but the groove also adds visual interest to an otherwise uninspiring slab of wood. To make this groove, cut a template from hardboard and secure it to the cutting board with double-faced carpet tape. Cut the groove with a guide collar and a core-box bit, keeping the collar firmly against the template.

For decorative grooves with a more complex geometry, you can make multiple passes — or use a more complex bit. For example, by making multiple parallel passes with a point-cut roundover bit (sometimes called a "beading" bit), you can form cock beads and reeds. (SEE FIGURE 4-15.) Or, make cuts with a veining bit or round-nose bit to create flutes. (SEE FIGURE 4-16.) A point-cut ogee bit will rout a wide groove with a double-ogee shape. (SEE FIGURE 4-17.)

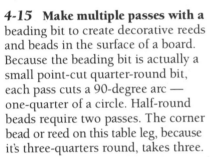

4-15 Make multiple passes with a beading bit to create decorative reeds and beads in the surface of a board. Because the beading bit is actually a small point-cut quarter-round bit, each pass cuts a 90-degree arc — one-quarter of a circle. Half-round beads require two passes. The corner bead or reed on this table leg, because it's three-quarters round, takes three.

4-16 A flute is just a half-round groove — the opposite of a half-round bead. Often, it's blind at one or both ends. Use a veining bit to cut the flute and a straightedge to guide the router. If the flute is blind, it also helps to have a plunge router. Attach stops to the straightedge to halt the cut when the flute is the proper length.

4-17 Point-cut bits with a complex shape, such as this pilotless ogee bit, cut a broad groove with an interesting shape. The sides of the grooves are mirror images of each other.

TRY THIS TRICK

Cut a set of grooves in a board, parallel to each other. Make each groove a little more than half as deep as the board thickness. Turn the board upside down and cut another set of grooves *at an angle to the first set.* Where the grooves intersect, they will create openings. The size, shape, and spacing of these openings depends on the size, shape, and spacing of the grooves. The finished product makes a great decorative panel, screen or trivet.

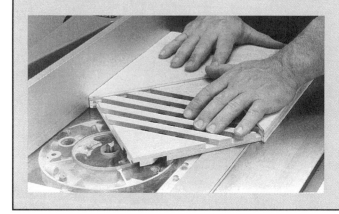

MAKING COMPLEX MOLDINGS

When you produce complex moldings, you often make multiple cuts, combining both edge and surface treatments. This isn't difficult, but there are a few tricks you should know.

The first trick is to decide which router bits to use to cut what shapes. Oftentimes this is more of an art than a science. There may be three or four bits in your selection that will produce a single shape. Knowing which one will work best is a matter of experience. Consult "Common Multiple-Cut Moldings" on page 85 for ideas.

Second, when you know which bits you're using, carefully plan the cuts. Each cut should leave enough stock to adequately support the workpiece during the next cut. If possible, make small cuts before large ones, and remove stock from the interior or middle of a surface before taking it from the sides. (*SEE FIGURE 4-18.*)

Third, when you make each cut, use constant, even pressure to feed the work (or move the router) and keep it firmly against the guides. If the pressure isn't constant or if the work wanders slightly, the cut may not be even. If the problem continues over several passes, there may be considerable variation in the molded shape along the length of the board.

Finally, make more molding than you think you'll need. If you run short, it will be difficult to reproduce exactly all the setups you went through.

4-18 When making a complex molding, plan the sequence of cuts so the stock remains as stable as possible. For instance, to cut this picture frame molding, rout the smaller quarter-round bead *before* the larger ogee. If you cut the ogee first, the stock may rock when you make the bead. Leave the rabbet until last. Having a solid edge on your workpiece will provide additional support as you hold it against the fence.

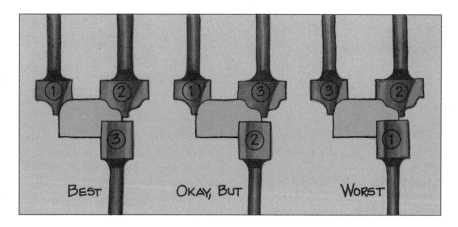

TRY THIS TRICK

Instead of making multiple passes to create a complex molding, glue up several simpler shapes. The easiest way to do this is to *laminate* the shapes — build them up in layers. But you can also *join* the shapes — cut dadoes, rabbets, or grooves in the molding stock, then glue smaller strips of wood in these joints. Furthermore, the strips that you glue together don't all have to be the same species. Glue up contrasting colors of wood, if you want.

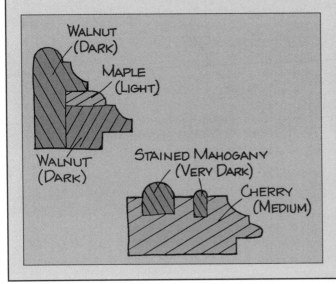

WALNUT
(DARK)

MAPLE
(LIGHT)

WALNUT
(DARK)

STAINED MAHOGANY
(VERY DARK)

CHERRY
(MEDIUM)

CUTTING DECORATIVE SHAPES WITH A SHAPER

EDGE TREATMENTS

Owing to the design of the machine, shapers are used mostly for edge treatments. You can rest the stock on its edge to cut the surface if you need to. However, because the spindle travels only a short distance, you can cut only a small portion of a board's face. A few manufacturers offer cutters to shape the face of 3½-inch-wide moldings, but these are for industrial machines with 1-inch-diameter spindles. In most home workshops, shapers are used only to cut the edges of workpieces.

The technique for shaping decorative edges is very similar to cutting them with a table-mounted router. Use a fence to guide stock with straight edges, and a rub collar and starting pin for contoured edges. Feed the work slowly against the rotation of the cutter and make two or more passes to create complex shapes. If necessary, use featherboards for hold-downs. (SEE FIGURE 4-19.) Don't try to shape small or slender stock; shape large boards, then cut them into smaller pieces.

There are important differences, however, between making a molding on a router and making it on a

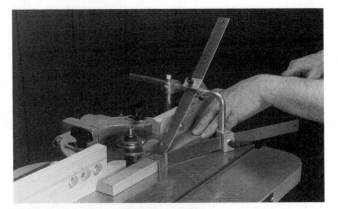

4-19 Several manufacturers offer spring hold-downs for shapers. These attach directly to a shaper fence and do the same job as featherboards. Both featherboards and hold-downs allow you to shape thin or narrow stock safely. There is a point, however, when the stock becomes too thin or too narrow, even if you use a hold-down. When the stock chips or splinters, it's too small to shape safely.

shaper. As mentioned before, a shaper can remove more stock in a single pass than a router can. You can also stack the cutters on the spindle of a shaper to produce useful or interesting combinations of shapes. (*SEE FIGURES 4-20 AND 4-21.*) And because you can reverse

the shaper's direction of rotation, you can use cutters right-side up *and* upside down. Many cutters are designed to take advantage of this capability, and have a different shape cut into each end. (*SEE FIGURES 4-22 AND 4-23.*)

4-20   You can cut complex shapes with multiple passes, but often you can save yourself time by stacking two or more shapes on a spindle and cutting them all at once. Here, a small bed shape is stacked on top of a quarter-round to create a unique table edge. (*Cutter guard removed for clarity.*)

4-21   By stacking a small crown molding cutter (part of a sash molding set) on a groove or jointer cutter, you can create a cabinet door lip with a crown shape, instead of the usual quarter-round. (*Cutter guard removed for clarity.*)

4-22   Some shaper cutters are designed to cut two different shapes, depending on the direction of rotation. Here, the cutter is mounted to cut a cove. The spindle will rotate counterclockwise. (*Cutter guard removed for clarity.*)

4-23   Flip the cutter end for end, reverse the rotation of the motor so it spins clockwise, and the same cutter will make a quarter-round bead. (*Cutter guard removed for clarity.*)

COMMON MULTIPLE-CUT MOLDINGS

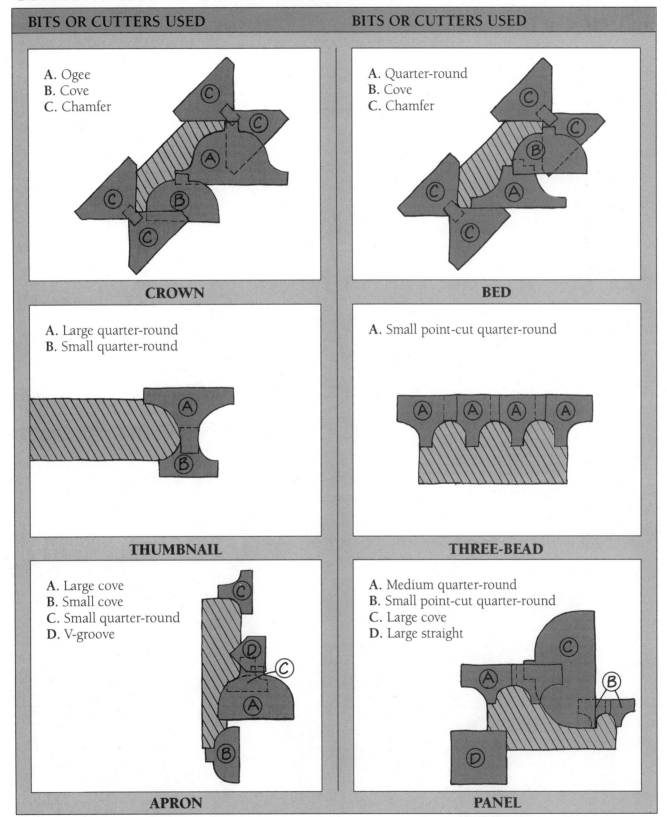

BITS OR CUTTERS USED

A. Ogee
B. Cove
C. Chamfer

CROWN

BITS OR CUTTERS USED

A. Quarter-round
B. Cove
C. Chamfer

BED

A. Large quarter-round
B. Small quarter-round

THUMBNAIL

A. Small point-cut quarter-round

THREE-BEAD

A. Large cove
B. Small cove
C. Small quarter-round
D. V-groove

APRON

A. Medium quarter-round
B. Small point-cut quarter-round
C. Large cove
D. Large straight

PANEL

CUTTING DECORATIVE SHAPES IN ROUND STOCK

In addition to routing flat surfaces, you can also cut decorative shapes in *round* stock, such as a lathe-turned spindle. This requires an overarm router (or an overhead routing jig) and a special V-jig with an indexing wheel to hold and calibrate the spindle.

Turn the spindle, leaving a tenon at each end. The tenons must be about 1 inch long *and* be exactly the same diameter. After routing the decorative shapes in the surface of the spindle, cut the tenons off on a band saw (if you don't need them).

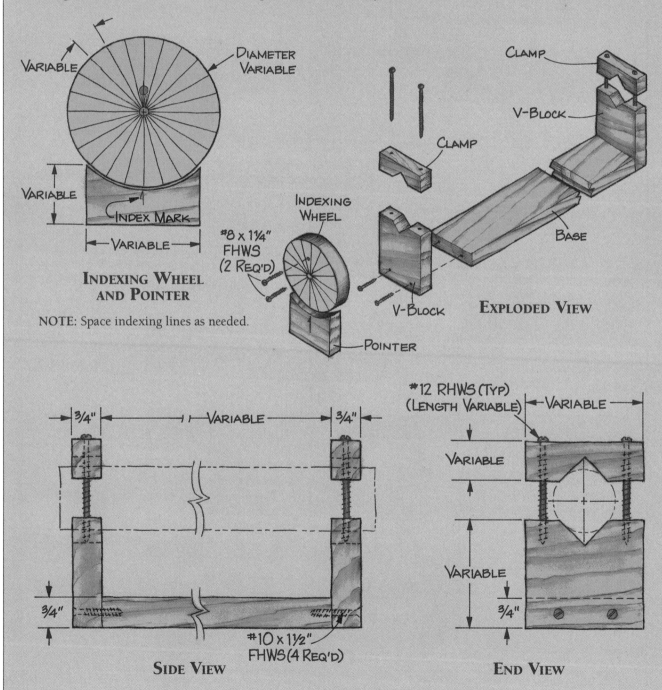

VARIABLE

DIAMETER VARIABLE

VARIABLE

INDEX MARK

VARIABLE

INDEXING WHEEL AND POINTER

NOTE: Space indexing lines as needed.

#8 x 1¼" FHWS (2 REQ'D)

INDEXING WHEEL

POINTER

V-BLOCK

CLAMP

CLAMP

V-BLOCK

BASE

EXPLODED VIEW

¾" | VARIABLE | ¾"

¾"

#10 x 1½" FHWS (4 REQ'D)

SIDE VIEW

#12 RHWS (TYP) (LENGTH VARIABLE)

VARIABLE

VARIABLE

VARIABLE

¾"

END VIEW

1 **Mount the spindle in the** V-jig and fasten the indexing wheel to the end of one tenon with two small screws. Rotate the spindle to align the index mark on the pointer with the first line on the wheel, then tighten the clamps.

2 **Clamp a straightedge to the** worktable, beneath the router. This will guide the jig as you feed the stock into the center of the bit. Position the straightedge so the axis of the spindle will pass directly beneath the bit.

3 **Turn the router on and feed** the spindle under the bit. As you do so, hold the jig firmly against the straightedge.

4 **After completing a cut, turn** the router off. Loosen the clamps and rotate the spindle to align the index mark with the next mark needed on the indexing wheel. Tighten the clamps and make another cut. Repeat until you have cut the shapes you want all around the circumference of the spindle.

ALTERNATIVE TOOLS

While routers and shapers are the most common tools for cutting molded shapes in wood, they are not the only tools for the job. In some cases, they may not be the best tools. There are several good alternatives and, under certain circumstances, one of these may work better for you than a router or a shaper.

For example, many craftsmen still prefer a *molding plane*, the ancestor of the router and the shaper. Once you acquire the knack, you can cut simple moldings and joints with this hand tool as quickly as you can with any power tool. Furthermore, a molding plane will not burn the wood and, in certain operations, offers better control than a power tool. Updated versions of these old-time planes are still available through most mail-order woodworking catalogues, as are interchangeable plane irons for cutting moldings and joints.

If you like hand tools, you might also try a scratch stock or *beading tool*. This looks like a spokeshave and works like a scraper — it scrapes a shape in the wood as you draw it across the surface. Like the molding plane, it has interchangeable blades to cut a variety of shapes. A beading tool leaves an extremely smooth surface, will not tear the grain, and is excellent for shaping small parts or figured wood.

WHERE TO FIND IT

Beading tools, sets of shaped blades, and blank blades (so you can grind your own shapes) are available from:

Lie-Nielsen Toolworks
Route 1
Warren, ME 04864

Finally, there are *molding heads* available for most table saws and some planers. This power tool accessory mounts on a saw or planer arbor, holding two or three shaped knives *horizontally*. Because of this — and because of the tool on which the accessory is mounted — the molding head is useful for cutting molded shapes in the faces of wide boards. Like the plane irons and the beading blades, the molding knives are interchangeable.

1 A beading tool cuts slowly but very smoothly. Draw it across the wood repeatedly with a steady, fluid motion. With each stroke, the blade, which is set nearly perpendicular to the wood, will scrape away a tiny amount of stock. After a few dozen strokes, the molded shape will appear.

2 Unlike the router and the shaper, which spin bits and cutters vertically, a molding head spins *horizontally*. This makes it especially useful for cutting shapes in the *faces* of boards.

PROJECTS

5

MINIATURE CHEST

For hundreds of years, before the Victorian inventions of jewelry boxes and file drawers, folks kept valuables and important papers in small chests. These were called, appropriately enough, "keeping boxes." This small chest is typical of many built in the late eighteenth and early nineteenth centuries, with one modern twist — all the joints and decorative moldings are made with a router or shaper.

Cut the through dovetails with the aid of a dovetail template, and the remaining joinery — lock joints, dadoes, rabbets, tongues, and grooves — with a table-mounted router. Use either a router or a shaper to mold the edges of the lid and feet.

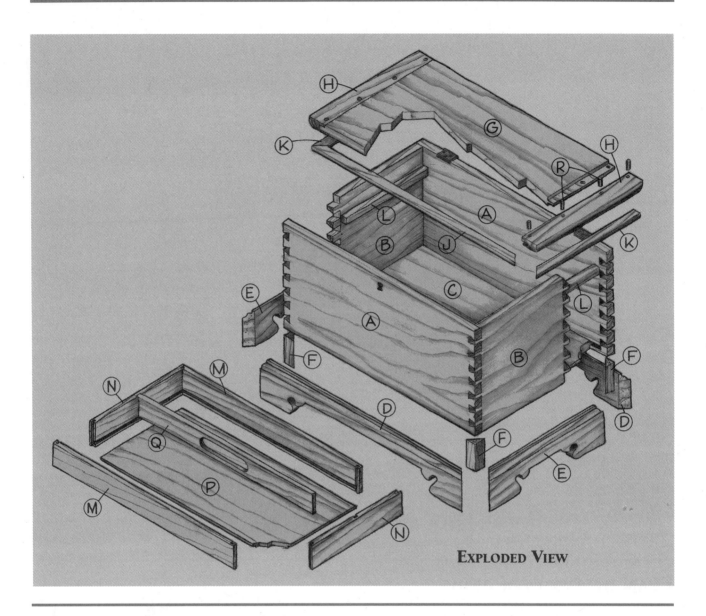

EXPLODED VIEW

MATERIALS LIST (FINISHED DIMENSIONS)

Parts

A. Front/back (2)   ½″ x 7½″ x 16″
B. Sides (2)   ½″ x 7½″ x 8″
C. Bottom   ½″ x 7⁷⁄₁₆″ x 15½″
D. Front/back
   feet (2)   ½″ x 2½″ x 17″
E. Side feet (2)   ½″ x 2½″ x 9″
F. Glue blocks (4)   ¾″ x ¾″ x 2″
G. Lid   ½″ x 8⅝″ x 15¾″
H. Breadboards
   (2)   ½″ x 1¼″ x 8⅝″
J. Front
   molding   ¼″ x ½″ x 17⅛″

K. Side
   moldings (2)   ¼ x ½″ x 8⁹⁄₁₆″
L. Ledgers (2)   ½″ x ½″ x 7″
M. Tray front/
   back (2)   ⅜″ x 1¾″ x 14⅝″
N. Tray
   sides (2)   ⅜″ x 1¾″ x 6⅞″
P. Tray
   bottom   ¼″ x 6⁵⁄₁₆″ x 14⅜″
Q. Tray
   divider   ⅜″ x 1½″ x 14⅜″
R. Pegs (8)   ¼″ dia. x ½″

Hardware

1″ x 2″ Brass butt hinges and
mounting screws (2)

Locking latch and mounting
screws (optional)

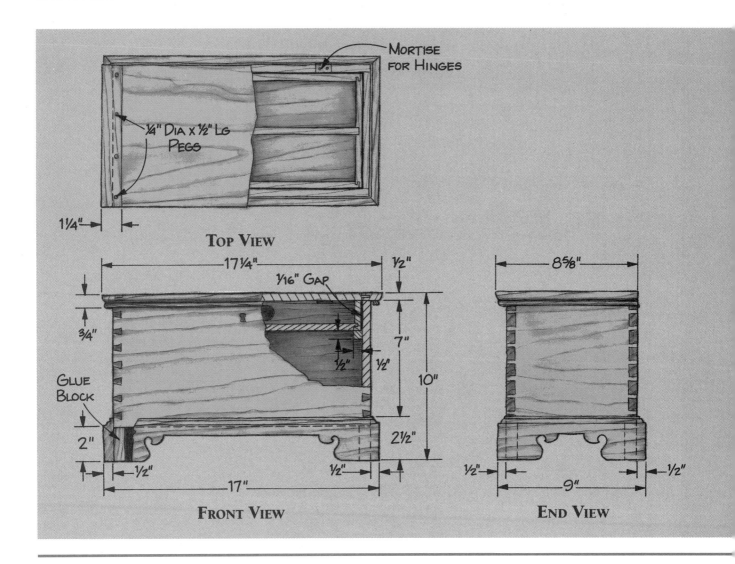

MORTISE FOR HINGES

¼" DIA X ½" LG PEGS

1¼"

TOP VIEW

17¼"

½"

1/16" GAP

¾"

½" ½"

7"

GLUE BLOCK

10"

2"

½"

2½"

17"

½"

½"

FRONT VIEW

8⅝"

½"

9"

½"

END VIEW

PLAN OF PROCEDURE

1 Select the stock and cut the parts to size.
To make this keeping box, you need about 9 board feet of 4/4 (four-quarters) stock. Historically, these boxes were built from mahogany, cherry, walnut, or maple. A few were made from white pine or poplar. However, you can use any cabinet-grade wood you fancy.

Plane the stock to ¾ inch thick and cut the glue blocks. Bevel the edges as shown in the *Glue Block Detail*. Plane the remaining stock to ½ inch thick and cut all the box parts to size, *except* the feet and moldings. Cut the feet to the width needed, but make them 1 to 2 inches longer than specified in the Materials List. Do not cut the moldings to width or length; just set aside some stock to make them later.

When you've cut the ½-inch-thick parts, plane the remaining stock to ⅜ inch and cut the tray front,

back, sides, and divider to size. Make a few extra tray sides to use as test pieces. Plane the remaining ⅜-inch-thick stock to ¼ inch and cut the tray bottom.

2 Rout the bottom joinery for the box and tray. The edges and ends of both the box bottom and the tray bottom are rabbeted. These rabbets form tongues which fit in grooves in the adjoining parts, as shown in the *Box Bottom Joinery* and *Tray Bottom Joinery* drawings.

Using a table-mounted router and a ¾-inch straight bit, cut a ¼-inch-wide, ¼-inch-deep rabbet around the perimeter of the box bottom. Cut a ⅛-inch-wide, ⅛-inch-deep rabbet around the perimeter of the tray bottom. This will create tongues on both parts as shown in the drawings.

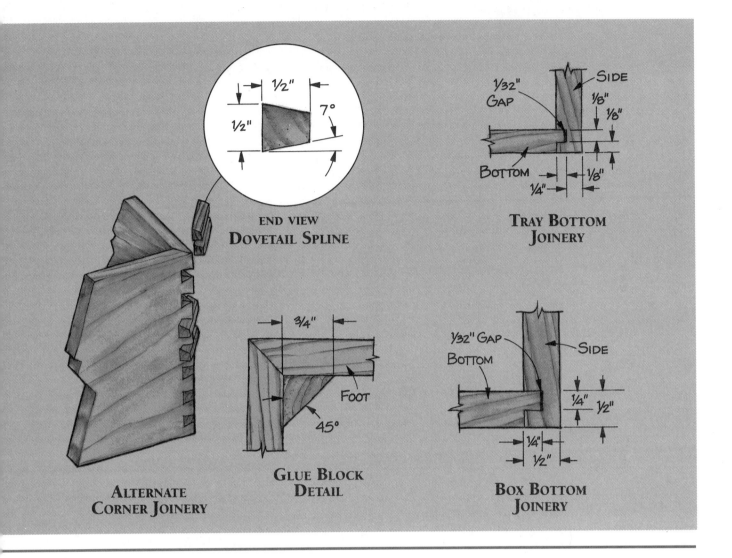

END VIEW
DOVETAIL SPLINE

½" ½" 7°

TRAY BOTTOM JOINERY

1/32" GAP SIDE 1/8" 1/8" BOTTOM ¼" 1/8"

ALTERNATE CORNER JOINERY

GLUE BLOCK DETAIL

¾" FOOT 45°

BOX BOTTOM JOINERY

1/32" GAP BOTTOM SIDE ¼" ½" ¼" ½"

Mount a ¼-inch straight bit in the table-mounted router. Using the fence to guide the board, rout ¼-inch-wide, ¼-inch-deep grooves in the box front, back, and sides. Make the grooves in the box parts *double-blind* — stop them ¼ inch before the ends of the boards. Otherwise, they'll show on the assembled project. Do *not* cut the ⅛-inch-wide, ⅛-inch-deep grooves in the tray parts yet.

3 Rout the dovetails in the box parts and assemble them. Using your router and a *through* dovetail jig, join the box front, back, and sides with through dovetails. Cut the tails in the front and back, and the pins in the sides.

If you plan to install a locking latch, rout a mortise for the lock in the inside face of the box front. Finish

sand the front, back, sides, and bottom. Assemble the front, back, and sides with glue. As you do, insert the bottom in its grooves, but do *not* glue it. When the glue dries, sand the dovetail joints clean and flush.

Alternatives — If you don't have a jig capable of making through dovetails, consider joining these parts with dovetail splines, as shown in the *Alternate Corner Joinery* drawing. Miter the adjoining ends of the front, back, and sides at 45 degrees. Join them with glue. As you do, insert the bottom in its grooves.

Using a dovetail spline jig, cut several dovetail-shaped grooves in the corners. Rout dovetail splines, cut them into short lengths, and glue them in the grooves. When the glue dries, cut and sand them flush with the surfaces of the box. (Refer to the "Dovetail Spline Jig" on page 66.)

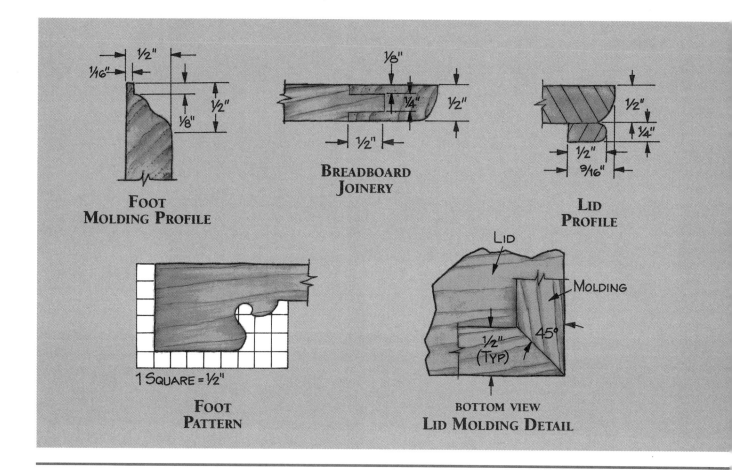

FOOT MOLDING PROFILE

BREADBOARD JOINERY

LID PROFILE

1 SQUARE = ½"

FOOT PATTERN

BOTTOM VIEW LID MOLDING DETAIL

4 Rout the molded ends on the feet. Using a table-mounted router and an ogee bit, rout an ogee-and-fillet in the top edge of the front, back, and side feet, as shown in the *Foot Molding Profile*.

5 Cut and assemble the feet. Measure the length and width of the assembled box. If these measurements have changed from what is shown in the drawings, adjust the lengths of the feet to compensate. Cut the feet to size, mitering the ends at 45 degrees.

Enlarge the *Foot Pattern* and trace it onto the stock. Cut the shapes of the feet with a band saw or scroll saw. Sand the sawed edges.

Finish sand the feet, then glue the parts together. Reinforce the miter joints with glue blocks. The bottom ends of these blocks must be flush with the bottom edges of the feet. When the glue dries, sand the joints clean and flush.

6 Attach the box to the feet. Finish sand the outside surfaces of the box and feet assemblies, as needed. Glue the box to the feet so the bottom surface of the box rests on the glue blocks that reinforce the feet.

7 Assemble the breadboards and the lid. Using a table-mounted router and a ¼-inch straight bit, rout a ¼-inch-wide, ½-inch-deep groove in the inside edges of the breadboards. Switch to a ½-inch straight bit and cut two ½-inch-wide, ⅛-inch-deep rabbets in each end of the lid. These rabbets will form tongues that fit the breadboard grooves.

Note: Craftsmen traditionally applied breadboards to the ends of box lids, table tops, and cutting boards to hide the end grain and prevent the wide boards from cupping. The term was borrowed from an old-time kitchen utensil — a large, wide board that was used to knead bread.

Temporarily assemble the lid and the breadboards. Drill ¼-inch-diameter holes through the tongue-and-groove joints, as shown in the *Top View*. Disassemble the pieces. Using a small round file, slightly elongate the holes in the tongues to create ⅜-inch-long slots. The long dimension of these slots should run *perpendicular* to the wood grain. (*SEE FIGURE 5-1.*)

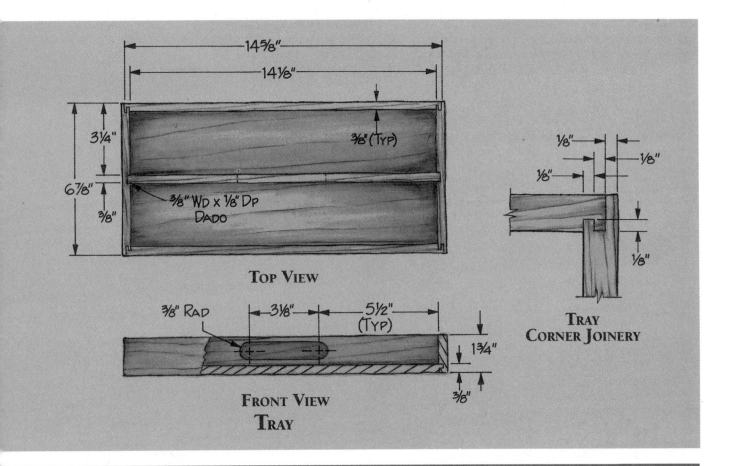

14⅝"

14⅛"

3¼"

⅜" (TYP)

6⅞"

⅜"

⅜" WD x ⅛" DP
DADO

TOP VIEW

⅛"

⅛"

⅛"

⅛"

**TRAY
CORNER JOINERY**

⅜" RAD

3⅛"

5½"
(TYP)

1¾"

⅜"

**FRONT VIEW
TRAY**

Reassemble the breadboards and the lid — do *not* glue the tongues in the grooves. Secure the parts with pegs, gluing the pegs in the holes. Try not to get any glue in the slots. The breadboards will help keep the lid from cupping, but the slots will let the lid expand and contract with changes in humidity.

Note: If you wish, you can glue the *middle* 2 inches of the lid tongues into the breadboard grooves. The lid will expand and contract from the middle out.

8 Fit the molding to the lid. Sand the surfaces of the lid, breadboards, and pegs flush. Using a ⅜-inch roundover bit in a table-mounted router, round-over the front and side edges of the lid assembly, as shown in the *Lid Profile*. Leave the back edge square.

Using a small beading or nosing bit, cut a half-round bead in the edge of the molding stock. Rip the ½-inch-wide moldings from the stock and cut them to length, mitering the adjoining ends. Finish sand the lid assembly and the moldings, then glue the moldings to the lid. (When the lid is attached to the box, these moldings should form a lip on three sides — right, left, and front.)

5-1 Using a file, enlarge the peg holes in the lid to create ¼-inch-wide, ⅜-inch-long slots that run perpendicular to the wood grain. This will allow the lid to expand and contract when it's pegged to the breadboards.

9 Attach the lid to the box. Using a straight bit and a small router (such as a laminate trimmer or miniature router), rout hinge mortises in the lid and back. If you're installing a locking latch, also cut a recess in the underside of the lid for the latch.

When cutting the mortises in the top edge of the back, mount the router on an oversize sole or the platform from "Making and Using an Overhead Routing Jig" on page 16. *(SEE FIGURE 5-2.)* After cutting the mortises, attach the hinges to the lid, then mount the lid to the box. Also install the lock and latch, if you've elected to do so.

10 Dado the tray sides for the tray divider. Using a 3/8-inch straight bit and a table-mounted router, cut 3/8-inch-wide, 1/8-inch-deep dadoes in the tray sides, as shown in the *Tray/Top View*. Use a miter gauge to guide the stock over the bit.

11 Cut the handle in the tray divider. Using a 3/4-inch-diameter straight bit in a table-mounted router, rout a slot in the tray divider, as shown in the *Tray/Front View*. This will create a cutout for the handle. Sand the routed edges of the cutout. If you wish, round-over these edges with a 1/4-inch roundover bit.

12 Rout the lock joints in the tray front, back, and sides. The front, back, and sides of the tray are joined by interlocking tongues and dadoes, commonly called lock joints. Cut these joints with a table-mounted router and a 1/8-inch spline cutter, as explained in "Special Router Joinery" on page 68. Also cut the 1/8-inch-wide, 1/8-inch-deep grooves for the tray bottom with this spline cutter.

13 Assemble the tray and ledgers. Finish sand all the parts of the tray, then assemble the front, back, sides, and divider with glue. As you do, insert the tray bottom in its grooves, but do *not* glue it in place. Let it float in the grooves. Allow the glue to dry, then sand all the joints clean and flush.

Glue the ledgers to the inside faces of the box sides. These ledgers should support the tray so the top edges are about 1/32 inch below the top edges of the box.

14 Finish the keeping box. Remove the lid from the box and the hinges from the lid. Also remove the lock and latch, if you've installed them. Set the hardware aside and do any necessary touch-up sanding. Apply a stain or finish to the keeping box and tray and let the finish dry. Rub it out, then reassemble the parts.

The box shown was colored with an updated version of a traditional chemical stain to make it appear old. Wet the surface of the wood with a dilute solution of nitric acid (10 percent). Gently warm the surface with a heat gun until the color changes to a dark brown. (The nitric acid gently "burns" the wood, forming a dark patina that would otherwise take decades to form.) Immediately sponge the wood with a weak solution of baking soda and water to neutralize the acid.

Let the surface of the wood dry. Give it a light sanding to smooth the raised grain, and seal it with several coats of orange shellac.

A SAFETY REMINDER

Wear protective goggles, a face mask, and rubber gloves when handling the nitric acid. Work outdoors and avoid breathing the fumes. At high concentrations, nitric acid will corrode metals and is hazardous to the eyes and skin.

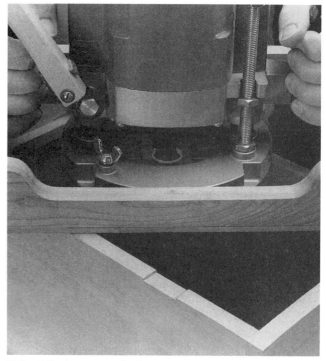

5-2 When cutting the hinge mortises in the back, use the platform from the overhead routing jig shown on page 16 to support the router. Otherwise, it will be difficult to balance the router on the narrow edge of the board.

6

ROUTER TABLE

If you use a router, you should have a router table. This accessory transforms your router from a portable power tool into a stationary one. In doing so, a router table increases the versatility and capability of the tool more than any single jig you can make or purchase. Furthermore, many routing operations are safer on a table-mounted router than they might be using a hand-held router.

This particular router table is designed to accommodate all sizes of routers, from the largest plunge routers to the smallest laminate trimmers and miniature routers. It's easy and economical to make. It incorporates all the necessary guides — fence, miter gauge slot, and starting pin. It also has a few unique features to make this table safer and easier to use. The work surface is laminate-covered for durability. The fence has a built-in dust collector to pick up sawdust while you're working. And the fence halves slide together or apart to accommodate all sizes of router bits.

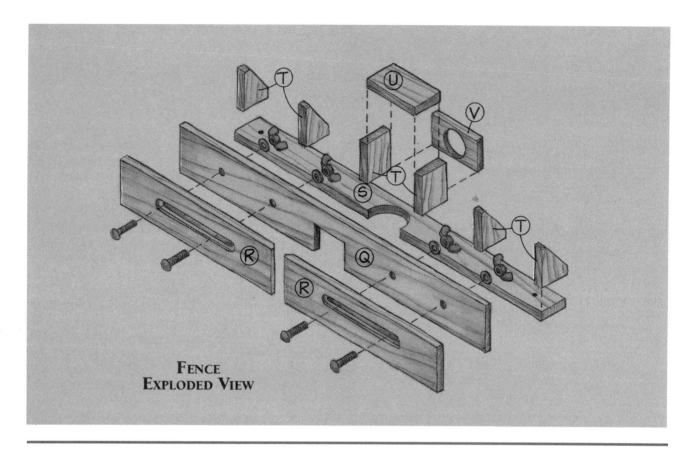

**FENCE
EXPLODED VIEW**

MATERIALS LIST (FINISHED DIMENSIONS)

Parts

Table

A. Worktable   ³/₄″ x 19¹/₂″ x 28¹/₂″
B. Front/back
    trim (2)   ³/₄″ x 1¹/₂″ x 30″
C. Side trim (2)   ³/₄″ x 1¹/₂″ x 21″
D. Front/back
    splines* (2)   ¹/₄″ x ³/₄″ x 28¹/₂″
E. Side
    splines* (2)   ¹/₄″ x ³/₄″ x 18³/₄″
F. Front/back
    aprons (2)   ³/₄″ x 1³/₄″ x 25¹/₄″
G. Side
    aprons (2)   ³/₄″ x 1³/₄″ x 14³/₄″
H. Wide legs (4)   ³/₄″ x 4″ x 13″
J. Narrow
    legs (4)   ³/₄″ x 3¹/₄″ x 13″
K. Table base* ³/₄″ x 13¹/₄″ x 22¹/₄″
L. Front/back
    base trim (2) ³/₄″ x ³/₄″ x 15¹³/₁₆″
M. Side base
    trim (2)   ³/₄″ x ³/₄″ x 6¹³/₁₆″

N. Front/back
    reinforcing frame   ³/₄″ x ³/₄″ x
    members (2)   (variable)
P. Side reinforcing
    frame   ³/₄″ x ³/₄″ x
    members (2)   (variable)

Fence

Q. Fixed face   ¹/₂″ x 4″ x 30″
R. Sliding faces (2)   ¹/₂″ x 4″ x 15″
S. Fence base*   ³/₄″ x 3″ x 30″
T. Braces* (6)   ³/₄″ x 3″ x 3¹/₄″
U. Dust collector
    top   ¹/₂″ x 3″ x 4¹/₂″
V. Dust collector
    back*   ³/₄″ x 2³/₄″ x 4¹/₂″

Make these parts from plywood.

Hardware

Table

#8 x 1¹/₄″ Flathead wood screws
(30–36)
#10 x 1¹/₂″ Roundhead wood
screws (14)
4d Finishing nails (12–16)
¹/₄″ or ³/₈″ Transparent acrylic
plastic (for mounting plate)
¹/₄″ x 2″ Steel starting pin

Fence

#8 x 1¹/₄″ Flathead wood screws
(12–16)
⁵/₁₆″ x 1¹/₂″ Carriage bolts (4)
⁵/₁₆″ x 2″ Carriage bolts (2)
⁵/₁₆″ Flat washers (6)
⁵/₁₆″ Wing nuts (6)

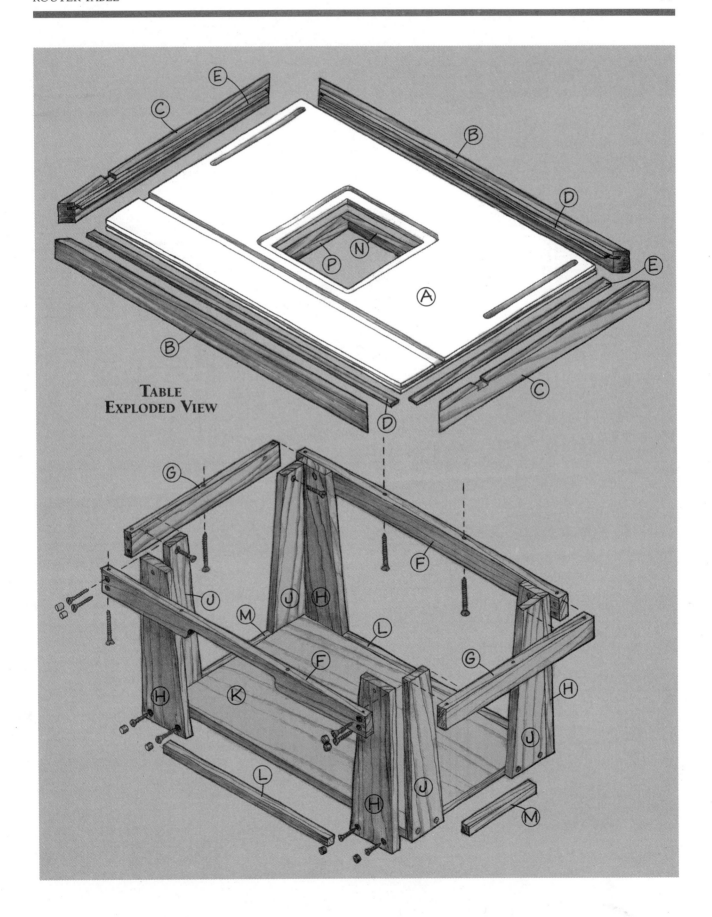

TABLE
EXPLODED VIEW

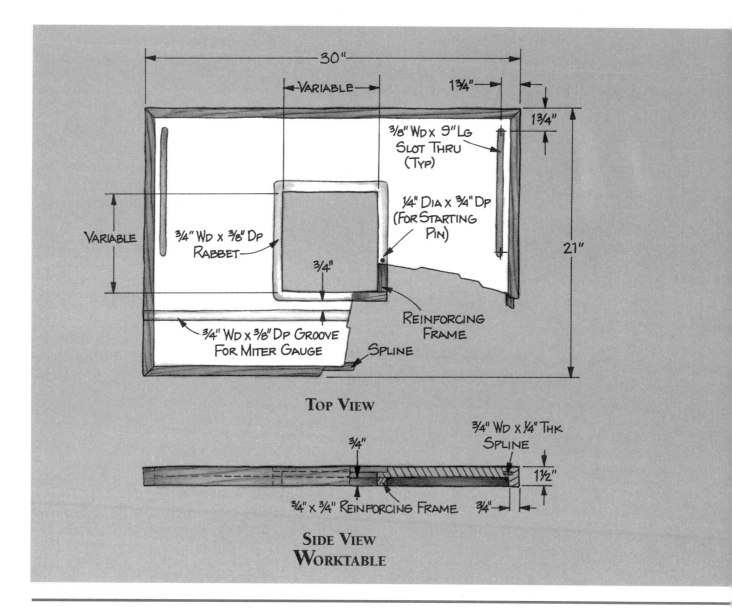

TOP VIEW

SIDE VIEW
WORKTABLE

PLAN OF PROCEDURE

MAKING THE TABLE

1 Select the stock and cut the table parts to size. To make this router table you need about 7 board feet of 4/4 (four-quarters) hardwood, a few scraps of ¼-inch and ¾-inch cabinet-grade plywood, and a laminate-covered sink cutout for the worktable. You can purchase a cutout at many home centers and lumberyards for less than it would cost you to make a worktable from scratch.

Cut the worktable, splines, and base to size. Plane the 4/4 stock to ¾ inch thick, and rip the trim, aprons, legs, and reinforcing frame members to the width needed. Cut the aprons and legs to length, but not the trim or frame members. (You'll cut these as you need them.) Set the remaining hardwood stock aside for the fence.

2 Rout the mounting plate mortise. Determine the size of the mounting plate needed for your router. Remember, this depends not only on the diameter of the router base, but also on the clearance needed for the handles, height clamp, and other router parts. Allow a little extra space for good measure.

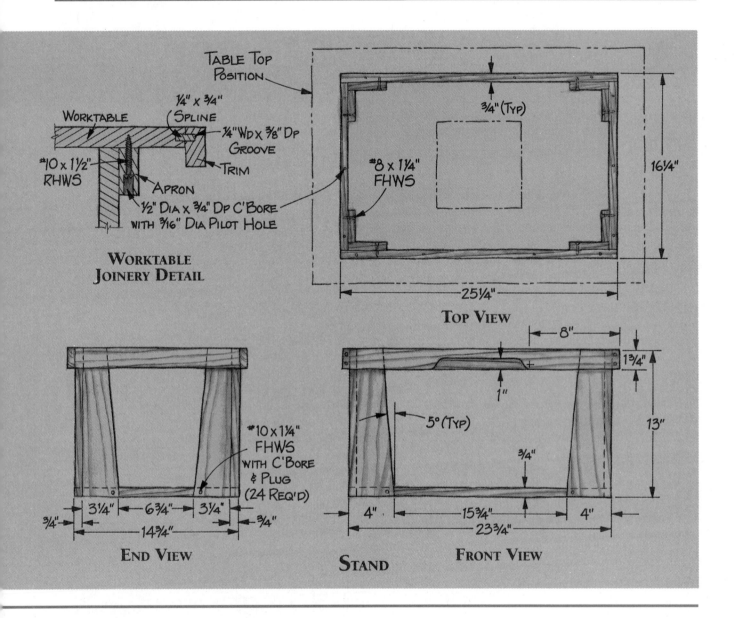

When you have decided on the dimensions, build a mortising frame and clamp it to the worktable. Mount a ³/₄-inch straight bit in your router. Using the frame to guide the router, rout a square groove in the worktable. The depth of the groove must be *precisely* the same as the thickness of the mounting plate stock. Using a saber saw to cut along the *inside* edges of the groove, remove the waste from the mortise and create an opening for the router. (See "Making a Mounting Plate" on page 12.)

3 Rout the fence slots. Lay out the fence mounting slots on the worktable. Mount a ³/₈-inch straight bit in the router, and clamp a straightedge to the worktable to serve as a guide. Rout two ³/₈-inch-wide, 9-inch-long slots through the table, as shown in the *Worktable/Top View*.

4 Attach the trim to the worktable. Using a ¹/₄-inch spline cutter bit, rout ¹/₄-inch-wide, ³/₈-inch-deep slots in the edges and ends of the table. Rout matching slots in the inside faces of the trim. **Note:** Some spline cutters make ½-inch-deep slots. You may have to adjust the width of the splines to compensate.

Fit the trim to the worktable, mitering the adjoining ends at 45 degrees. Glue the trim to the worktable, using plywood splines to reinforce the glue joints, as shown in the *Worktable Joinery Detail*. Let the glue dry, then carefully scrape the top edges of the trim so it is flush with the worktable. Sand the miter joints smooth.

5 **Attach the reinforcing frame to the worktable.** Cut the reinforcing frame members to size, and glue them to the underside of the worktable. The inside edges of these frame members must be flush with the inside edges of the router opening.

6 **Cut the shape of the front apron.** Lay out the relief on the front apron stock, as shown in the *Stand/Front View*. (This relief will make it easier to change bits when the router is mounted to the table.) Cut the relief with a saber saw or band saw. Sand the sawed edges.

7 **Drill the mounting holes in the aprons.** Drill ½-inch-diameter, ¾-inch-deep counterbores in the *bottom* edges of the aprons, as shown in the *Stand/Top View* and *Worktable Joinery Detail*. Then drill ³⁄₁₆-inch-diameter pilot holes through the centers of these counterbores.

8 **Taper the legs.** Using a tapering jig, cut a 5-degree taper in the *inside* edges of the legs, as shown in the *Stand/Front View* and *Stand/End View*. (SEE FIGURE 6-1.) You can also cut rough tapers on a band saw, then smooth them on a jointer.

9 **Assemble the stand.** Glue the wide legs to the narrow legs to make four L-shaped "bracket" legs. Glue the aprons together to make a frame, and reinforce the corners with flathead wood screws. Counterbore and countersink the screws.

Glue and screw the legs to the outside edges of the base. Then glue and screw the legs to the inside faces of the apron assembly. Again, counterbore and countersink the screws.

If you wish, glue wooden plugs in the counterbores to hide the screw heads. Let the glue dry, then sand all joints and plugs flush.

10 **Fit and attach the trim to the base.** Cut the base trim to fit between the legs, mitering the ends at 85 degrees. Glue the trim to the base, and reinforce it with finishing nails. Set the heads of the nails. Sand the surfaces of the trim flush with the surfaces of the base and legs.

11 **Attach the stand to the worktable.** Turn the worktable and the stand assemblies upside down on your bench. Center the stand on the worktable. Drive roundhead screws through the mounting holes into the worktable.

12 **Attach the mounting plate to the table.** Cut a router mounting plate from transparent acrylic plastic. Make it about ¹⁄₃₂ inch larger than the mortise, then round the corners and shave the sides with a sander or a file until it fits snugly. Secure the plate to the worktable with flathead wood screws. Countersink these screws so the heads are slightly below the surface of the plate.

13 **Rout a miter gauge slot.** Lay out a miter gauge slot ¾ inch in front of the mounting plate, as shown in the *Worktable/Top View*. Mount a ¾-inch straight bit in your router. Clamp a straightedge to the worktable to guide the router, and rout a ¾-inch-wide, ³⁄₈-inch-deep slot from one end of the table to the other.

Note: *Most* (but not all) miter gauge bars are machined to fit a ¾-inch-wide, ³⁄₈-inch-deep slot. If yours is an odd size, adjust the dimensions of the slot accordingly.

6-1 Use a tapering jig and a table saw to cut the tapers in the legs. Using a protractor to measure the angle, adjust the jig to cut a 5-degree taper. Place the leg in the jig, then guide it along the fence, past the blade.

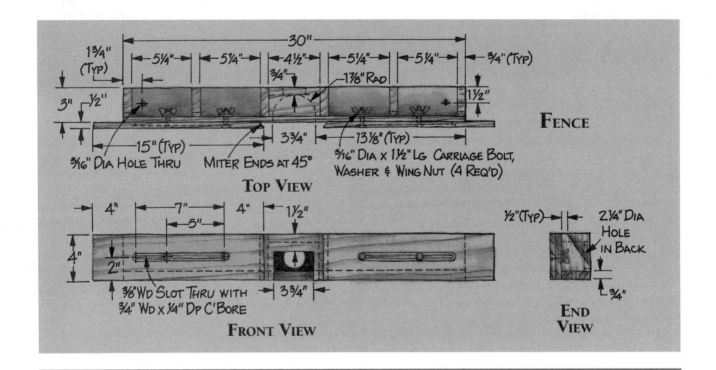

FENCE

TOP VIEW

FRONT VIEW

END VIEW

MAKING THE FENCE

14 Cut the fence parts to size. Cut the fence base, braces, and dust collector back to size. Plane the remaining 3/4-inch-thick hardwood stock to 1/2 inch and cut the fence faces and dust collector back. Miter the *inside* ends of the faces as shown in the *Fence/Top View*.

15 Taper the braces. Using a table saw or band saw, cut tapers in the four *outside* braces, as shown in the *Fence/End View*. Sand the sawed edges smooth.

16 Cut the shape of the base and fixed face. Lay out the cutouts in the fence base and fixed face, as shown in the *Fence/Front View* and *Fence/Top View*. Cut the shapes with a band saw or saber saw, and sand the sawed edges.

17 Drill holes in the base, fixed face, and dust collector back. Lay out the locations of the mounting bolts on the fence base and fixed face. Drill 5/16-inch-diameter holes for these bolts. Also, lay out the location of the 2 1/4-inch-diameter hole in the dust collector back. Cut this with a hole saw.

18 Rout slots in the sliding faces. Mount a 3/4-inch straight bit in your router, and secure the router to the router table. Clamp a straightedge to the worktable to guide the work (since the fence isn't

completed yet). Rout a 3/4-inch-wide, 1/4-inch-deep, 7 3/4-inch-long slot in the front surface of each sliding fence face. Switch to a 3/8-inch straight bit and — without changing the position of the straightedge — rout 3/8-inch-wide, 7 3/8-inch-long slots centered in the 3/4-inch-wide slots, as shown in the *Fence/Front View*.

19 Assemble the fence. Glue together the dust collector top, dust collector back, and two inside braces. Let the glue set up, then glue together the dust collector assembly, outside braces, fence base, and fixed face. Reinforce the glue joints with flathead wood screws. Countersink the screws.

Attach the sliding faces to the fixed fence face with carriage bolts, washers, and wing nuts. Attach the fence to the router table in the same manner.

FINISHING UP

20 Finish the table and fence. Remove the fence from the table and detach the sliding fence faces from the fence assembly. Remove the table frame from its stand, and set all hardware aside. Do any necessary touch-up sanding on the wood surfaces, then apply several coats of a *penetrating* finish, such as tung oil or Danish oil. Let the finish dry and buff it out with paste wax.

7

JOINT-MAKING JIG

Some routing tasks are easier (and safer) if you mount the router *beside* your work, holding the bit *horizontally*. This is particularly handy when making mortises, tenons, tongues, grooves, and other joints that require you to cut the edge of a board. With the router on its side, you can rest a work-piece on its face so it is better supported. You'll also find it easier to see what you're routing.

The jig shown holds the router horizontally beside a worktable. By pivoting the board on which the router is mounted, you adjust the height of the bit above (or below) the worktable. The jig includes a slot to hold a miter gauge when you need to rout the ends of boards. You can attach a standard-size vacuum hose to collect the sawdust as you cut.

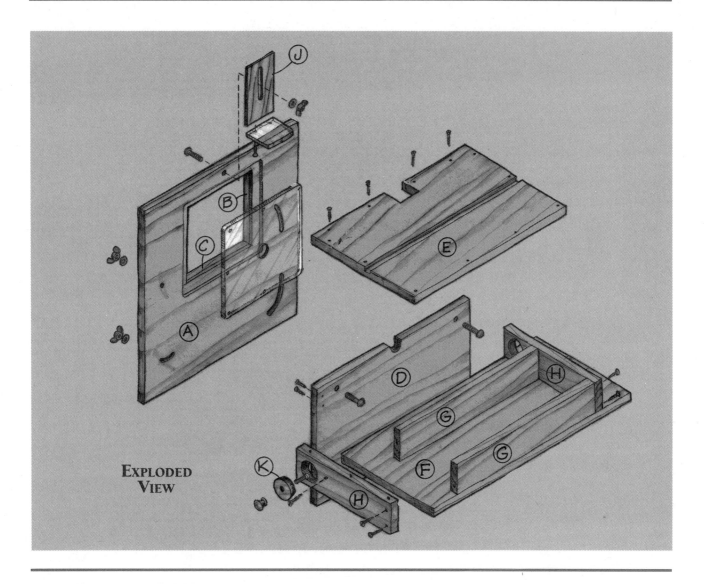

EXPLODED
VIEW

MATERIALS LIST (FINISHED DIMENSIONS)

Parts

A. Router
   mount   3/4" x 18" x 19 1/2"
B. Long cleats (2)   3/4" x 3/4" x 9 1/2"
C. Short cleats (2)   3/4" x 3/4" x 8"
D. Pivot plate   3/4" x 11 3/4" x 18"
E. Worktable   3/4" x 12" x 18"
F. Base   3/4" x 11 1/4" x 24"
G. Long
   supports (2)   3/4" x 3" x 16 1/2"
H. Short
   supports (2)   3/4" x 3" x 11 1/4"
J. Guard mount   3/8" x 3" x 6"
K. Dust collector
   plug   2 9/32" dia. x 3/4"

Hardware

Transparent acrylic plastic (for
   mounting plate and guard),
   1/4" or 3/8" x 10" x 14"
#6 x 3/4" Flathead wood screws (2)
#8 x 1 1/4" Flathead wood screws
   (30–36)
3/8" x 1 1/2" Carriage bolt
3/8" x 2" Carriage bolts (4)
3/8" Flat washers (5)
3/8" Wing nuts (5)
1 1/4" Drawer pull and mounting
   screw

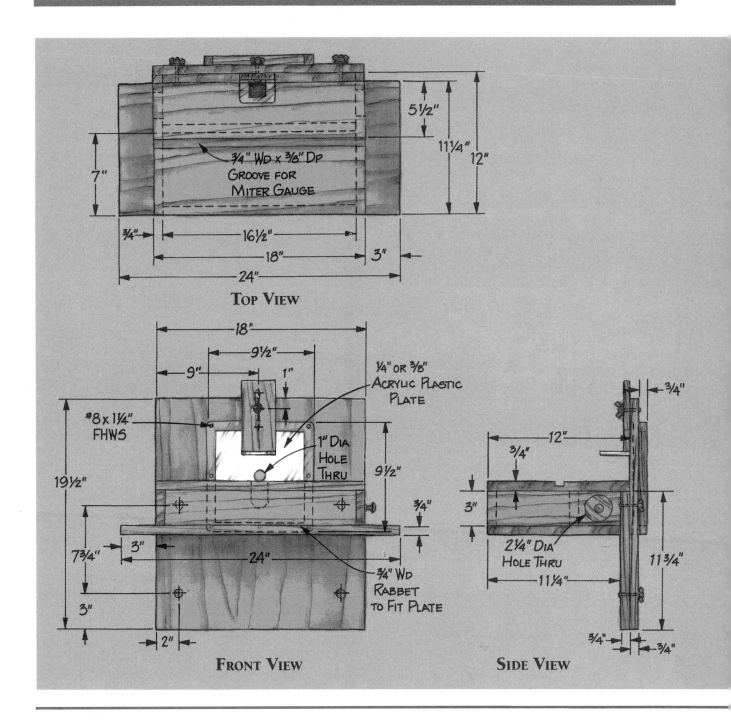

TOP VIEW

¾" WD x ⅜" DP
GROOVE FOR
MITER GAUGE

5½"
11¼"
12"
7"
¾"
16½"
18"
3"
24"

FRONT VIEW

18"
9½"
9"
1"
¼" OR ⅜"
ACRYLIC PLASTIC
PLATE
#8 x 1¼"
FHWS
1" DIA
HOLE
THRU
9½"
¾"
19½"
7¾"
3"
24"
3"
2"
¾" WD
RABBET
TO FIT PLATE

SIDE VIEW

¾"
12"
¾"
3"
2¼" DIA
HOLE THRU
11¼"
11¾"
¾"
¾"

PLAN OF PROCEDURE

1   Select the stock and cut the parts to size.   To
make the joint-making jig, you'll need a few ¾-inch-
thick scraps of hardwood and a 4 x 4-foot sheet of
very flat ¾-inch-thick material. On the jig shown, the
worktable is made from MDF (medium-density fiber-
board). The remaining parts are made from Baltic
birch plywood, a strong, flat imported plywood available by special order from most lumberyards. You
might also use laminate-covered particleboard for
the worktable and/or router mount.

When you have gathered the materials, cut all
the parts except the cleats to the sizes shown in the
Materials List. You will cut the cleats after you've
made the router mount.

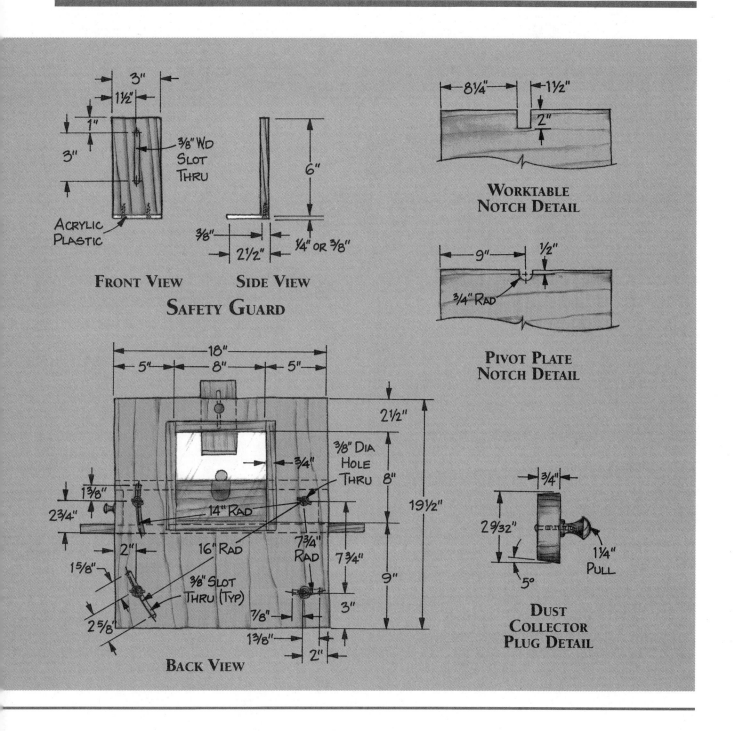

WORKTABLE NOTCH DETAIL

PIVOT PLATE NOTCH DETAIL

3/8" WD SLOT THRU

ACRYLIC PLASTIC

FRONT VIEW   **SIDE VIEW**

SAFETY GUARD

3/8" DIA HOLE THRU

14" RAD

16" RAD

3/8" SLOT THRU (TYP)

7 3/4" RAD

BACK VIEW

DUST COLLECTOR PLUG DETAIL

1 1/4" PULL

2   Rout the mortise in the router mount. The router is fastened to an acrylic plastic mounting plate, which is mortised into the router mount. As shown, this plate is 9½ inches square, large enough to accommodate almost any router and to allow good visibility from either side of the jig. To mount a very small router, you can use ¼-inch-thick plastic, but if the machine is over 1 horsepower, use ³/₈-inch-thick plastic.

Build a mortising frame and clamp it to the router mount. Install a ¾-inch straight bit in your router. Using the frame to guide the router, cut a groove in the mount, 9½ inches square. The depth of the groove must be *precisely* the same as the thickness of the

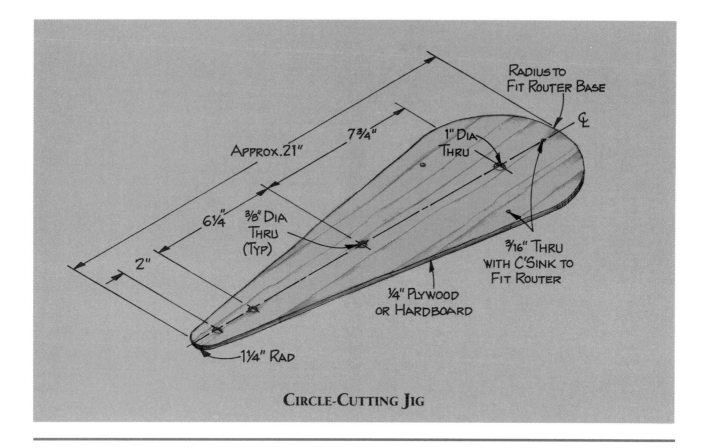

RADIUS TO
FIT ROUTER BASE

C̸L

1" DIA
THRU

APPROX.21"

7¾"

6¼"

⅜" DIA
THRU
(TYP)

2"

3/16" THRU
WITH C'SINK TO
FIT ROUTER

¼" PLYWOOD
OR HARDBOARD

1¼" RAD

CIRCLE-CUTTING JIG

mounting plate stock. Using a saber saw to cut along the *inside* edges of the groove, remove the waste from the mortise and create an opening for the router. (Refer to "Making a Mounting Plate" on page 12.)

Note: You can make a smaller mounting plate, if you wish. However, the center of the plate (where the bit protrudes) must be precisely where it is shown on the drawings.

3 Drill holes in the router mount and pivot plate.   Stack the pivot plate on the router mount so the sides and bottom edges are flush. Tape the two parts together to keep them from shifting, and mark the positions of the ⅜-inch-diameter holes on the pivot plate, as shown in the *Back View.* Drill all four of these holes through both the plate and the mount. Also, drill a hole in the router mount for the bolt that holds the guard.

4 Rout the curved slots in the router mount. Three of the holes in the router mount must be elongated to ⅜-inch-wide *curved* slots. The one hole that won't be enlarged serves as the pivot point for routing the three slots.

To rout the slots, first make the *Circle-Cutting Jig* shown. (This is similar to the *Large-Circle-Cutting Jig* on page 39.) Cut the jig from a scrap of ¼-inch plywood, drill it, and mount it to the base of your router.

Put a ⅜-inch straight bit in the router, and place a dowel center in the upper right-hand hole (as you face the *back* of the router mount). This will become the pivot hole for the circle-cutting jig. Insert the router bit in the lower left-hand hole, rotate the arm of the jig until it's over the dowel center, and press down firmly. The dowel center will leave a mark on the underside of the circle-routing jig. Repeat for the two right-hand holes, then drill ⅜-inch-diameter holes through the jig at the marks.

Mark the router mount to show where each slot should begin and end, as shown on the *Back View.* Note that each slot is a different length. (The farther from the pivot hole, the longer the slot.) Adjust the router's depth of cut to about ⅛ inch. Insert a ⅜-inch carriage bolt through the pivot hole and the hole in the jig that's closest to the router. Secure it with a washer and a wing nut. Don't tighten the nut too much; you must be able to pivot the arm.

Lift the router and the jig off the router mount.

(The plywood will flex slightly.) Turn the router on and lower it into the lower left-hand hole in the mount. Swing it clockwise a short distance, then back counterclockwise, cutting a curved slot. (*SEE FIGURE 7-1.*) Readjust the depth of cut, and rout the slot about ⅛ inch deeper. Repeat until you've cut the slot all the way through the router mount. Cut the remaining slots in the same manner.

5 **Rout the slot in the guard mount.** The guard mount has a single ⅜-inch-wide straight slot down the center. This lets you raise, lower, or tilt it at any angle. You can also rotate it up out of the way when changing bits. Cut this slot on a router table with a ⅜-inch straight bit. Remember, the slot is blind — halt the cut before you rout through to the ends.

6 **Cut the notches in the pivot plate and worktable.** Both the pivot plate and the worktable are notched so you can lower the router bit beneath the surface of the table. These notches also allow sawdust to fall down beneath the work surface, where it won't interfere with the work. Cut the notches with a saber saw or coping saw, as shown in the *Pivot Plate Notch Detail* and *Worktable Notch Detail*. Sand the sawed edges.

7 **Rout a miter gauge slot in the worktable.** Lay out a miter gauge slot 5½ inches from the pivot plate edge, as shown in the *Top View*. Mount a ¾-inch straight bit in your router. Clamp a straightedge to

the worktable to guide the router, and cut a ¾-inch-wide, ⅜-inch-deep slot from one end of the table to the other.

Note: *Most* (but not all) miter gauge bars are machined to fit a ¾-inch-wide, ⅜-inch-deep slot. If yours is an odd size, adjust the dimensions of the slot accordingly.

8 **Cut the dust collector ports.** Both of the short supports have a 2¼-inch-diameter hole near the pivot plate end, as shown in the *Side View.* These holes serve as dust collector ports — you can fit a vacuum hose with a standard 2¼-inch nozzle to them. They also serve as access holes to insert the two top mounting bolts through the pivot plate. Cut these holes with a hole saw.

9 **Make a plug for the dust collector holes.** When you use this jig, you only need to hook the vacuum to *one* of the ports — whichever location interferes least with the work. The other port must be plugged.

To make the plug, trace one of the holes on a scrap of ¾-inch-thick wood. Tilt the table of a band saw or scroll saw to 5 degrees. Saw the circle, cutting slightly outside the line so the plug will be about 1⁄32 inch oversize. Sand the sawed edge, then attach a drawer pull to the outside face of the plug, as shown in the *Dust Collector Plug Detail.* The plug should fit in each dust collector port like a cork.

7-1 Rout the curved slots in the router mount with a shop-made circle-routing jig. Use the upper left-hand hole in the mount as the pivot point for this jig.

10 **Assemble the jig.** Lightly sand all the surfaces to make sure they're clean. Cut the reinforcing cleats to size, and glue them to the back side of the router mount. The inside edges of these cleats must be flush with the inside edges of the router opening. If not, file the edges.

Assemble the worktable, pivot plate, supports, and base with glue and #8 flathead wood screws. Let the glue dry, then sand all the joints clean and flush.

Attach the plastic guard to the guard holder with #6 screws. Round the outside corners of the guard with a file.

USING THE JOINT-MAKING JIG

To use the joint-making jig, clamp the base to your workbench so the pivot plate hangs over one edge. Remove the router mount, fasten your router to the mounting plate, and replace the mount. Attach a shop vacuum to the jig and mount a bit in the router.

1 **Before each operation, you** must first make two adjustments — the bit height, and depth of cut. To adjust the height of the bit above the table, loosen the wing nuts that hold the router mount to the jig, rotate the mount up or down, and tighten the bolts. To adjust the depth of cut — how far the bit protrudes from the mount — slide the router in or out of its base and secure the height clamp. Also remember to adjust the guard.

2 **When cutting the edges of** boards, place the work flat on the worktable. Keep one edge pressed against the router mount as you feed the wood past the bit. Always feed the work against the rotation of the bit.

11 Finish the joint-making jig. Do any necessary touch-up sanding on the wood surfaces, then apply several coats of a *penetrating* finish, such as tung oil or Danish oil. Let the finish dry and buff it out with paste wax. Apply several coats of wax, carefully buffing each one. This will help the work slide smoothly across the worktable and the router mount.

12 Attach the router mount and guard. Insert 2-inch-long carriage bolts through all four holes in the pivot plate. Place the router mount over these bolts, put flat washers and wing nuts on the bolts, then hand-tighten the wing nuts. Insert a 1½-inch-long carriage bolt through the hole near the top of the router mount. Fit the guard assembly over this bolt and secure it with a washer and a wing nut.

Note: You can use almost any type of router bit with this jig, but you'll get better results with *shear-cut* or *spiral-cut* bits. These leave a cleaner cut and help to clear the sawdust as you work. Spiral bits also let you use the jig to bore horizontal holes.

3 To cut the end of a board, use the miter gauge to guide the wood past the bit. Keep the end of the board pressed against the router mount. Note that for this cut, part of the bit is *below* the surface of the table. For safety, never cut with the bit above the stock.

4 To make a plunge cut (as when starting a mortise), place the wood at an angle on the worktable. Rest one edge against the arris of the router mount, and place the area to be routed beside the bit. Holding the edge firmly against the mount, pivot the workpiece into the bit.

8

CANDLESTAND

Have you ever wondered why most candlestands have three legs? In days gone by, these stands were moved around often to adjust the lighting. Because they held candles and lamps, the stands had to sit solidly on the floor no matter where they were placed. Otherwise, they might have tipped over and started fires. A four-legged stand wobbles on an uneven floor, but three legs are always steady, no matter what the surface.

Old-time candlestands were built by hand, but much of the woodworking for this stand was done with a router. The legs are joined to the pedestal with sliding dovetails, cut with a router and dovetail bit. The round top was cut and the edge shaped with a router and the *Large-Circle-Cutting Jig* shown on page 39. The edges of both the legs and the top were rounded-over on a router table.

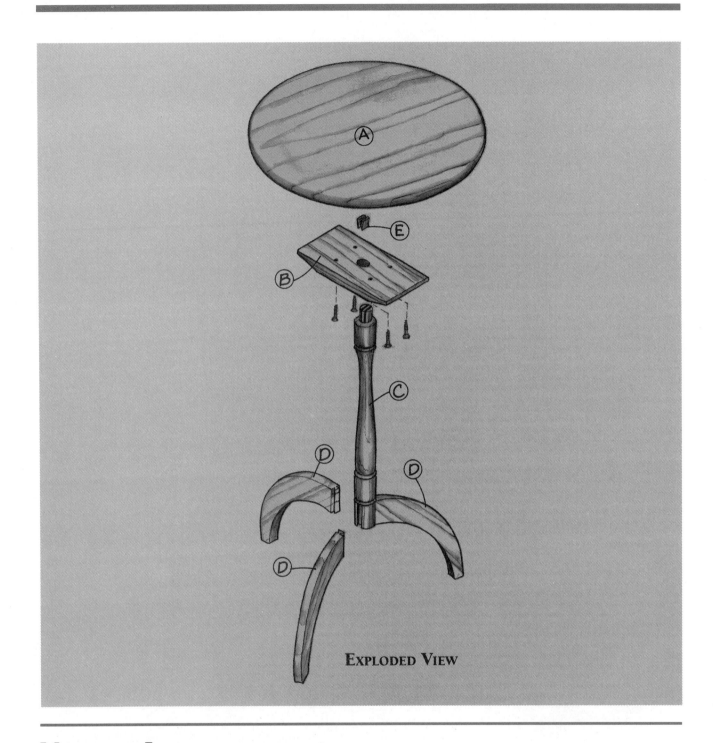

EXPLODED VIEW

MATERIALS LIST (FINISHED DIMENSIONS)

Parts

A. Tabletop $^3/_4$" x 18" dia.
B. Brace $^3/_4$" x 4" x 14"
C. Pedestal   2" dia. x 19$^3/_4$"
D. Legs (3) $^3/_4$" x 3$^3/_4$" x 12"
E. Wedges (2) $^5/_{32}$" x $^3/_4$" x 1"

Hardware

#8 x 1" Flathead wood screws (4)

PLAN OF PROCEDURE

1 **Select the stock and cut the parts to size.** To make this project, you need approximately 4 board feet of 4/4 (four-quarters) stock and an 8/4 (eight-quarters) turning block about 24 inches long. You can use almost any cabinet-grade hardwood — the candlestand shown is made from bird's-eye and curly maple.

Plane the 4/4 stock to ³/₄ inch thick, then cut the legs and brace to the sizes shown in the Materials List. Glue stock edge to edge to make a wide board for the top, and cut this about 1 inch longer and wider than specified. Cut the pedestal stock to length, but don't bother planing or cutting it to the stated thickness and width. Leave the turning block square. And don't cut the wedges until later.

2 **Rout the dovetail slots in the pedestal.** On the lathe, turn the pedestal to a simple cylinder, 2 inches in diameter. Turn the bottom portion of the cylinder (where you will attach the legs) to 1³/₄ inches in diameter.

Make the *V-Block Jig* shown. Mount the cylinder in the V-block and rout three ¹/₂-inch-wide, ¹/₂-inch-deep, 2¹/₂-inch-long dovetail slots in its bottom portion, as shown in the *Leg-to-Pedestal Joinery* drawing. Then rout a flat on top of each of these slots. (*SEE FIGURES 8-1 THROUGH 8-3.*)

8-1 **Before mounting the pedestal** stock in the V-block, make an indexing wheel as described in "Cutting Decorative Shapes in Round Stock" on page 86. Attach this to the *top* of the spindle. Place the stock loosely in the block and turn the stock until the first mark on the wheel aligns with the square. Tighten the straps.

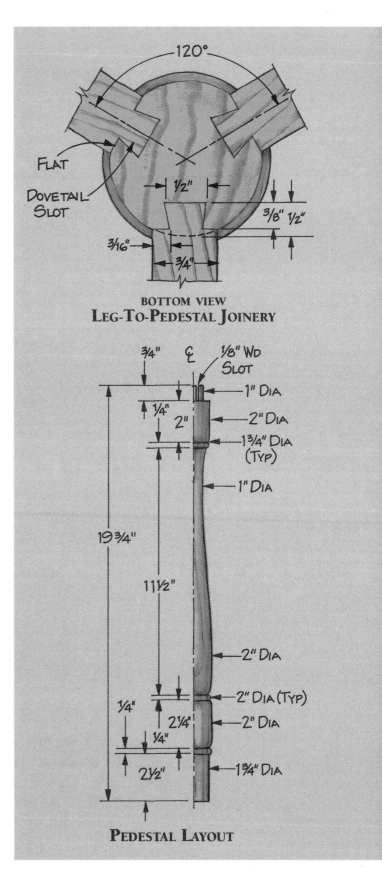

BOTTOM VIEW
LEG-TO-PEDESTAL JOINERY

PEDESTAL LAYOUT

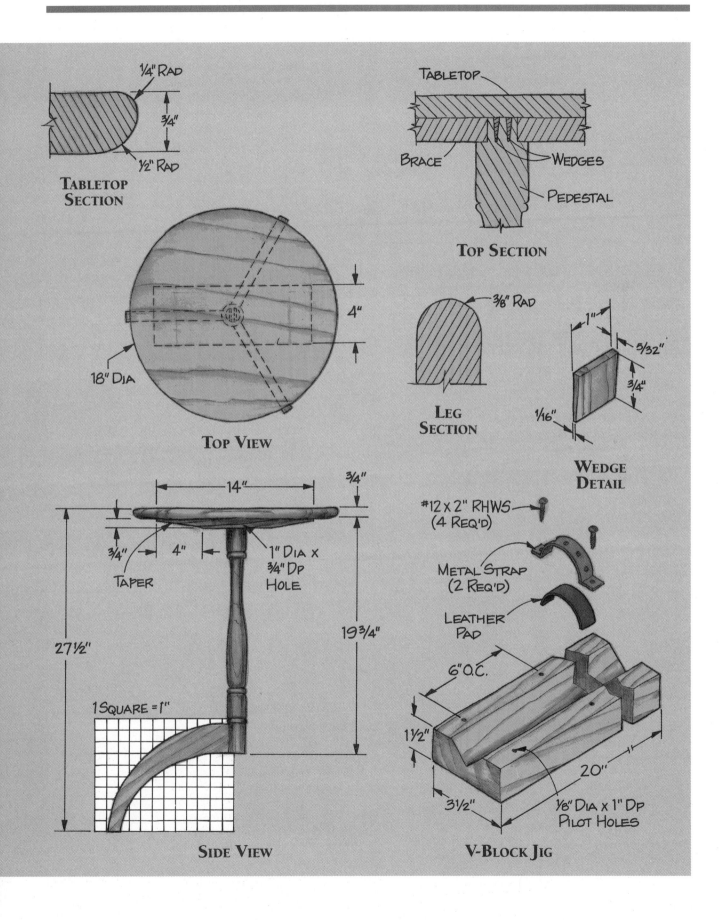

TABLETOP SECTION

¼" RAD

¾"

½" RAD

TOP VIEW

18" DIA

4"

SIDE VIEW

14"

¾"

¾"

4"

TAPER

1" DIA X ¾" DP HOLE

27½"

19¾"

1 SQUARE = 1"

TOP SECTION

TABLETOP

BRACE

WEDGES

PEDESTAL

LEG SECTION

⅜" RAD

WEDGE DETAIL

1"

5/32"

¾"

1/16"

#12 X 2" RHWS (4 REQ'D)

METAL STRAP (2 REQ'D)

LEATHER PAD

V-BLOCK JIG

6" O.C.

1½"

20"

3½"

⅛" DIA X 1" DP PILOT HOLES

3 Cut the shape of the legs. Enlarge the leg pattern in the *Side View* and trace it onto the leg stock. Using a band saw or scroll saw, cut the shape of the legs. Sand the sawed edges.

> ## FOR BEST RESULTS
>
> **S**tack the three leg boards face to face, and hold them together with double-faced carpet tape. Saw and sand all three legs at once, then remove the tape.

4 Cut the dovetail tenons in the legs. Put the same dovetail bit you used to make the slots in a table-mounted router. Rout a ½-inch-wide, ⅜-inch-long dovetail tenon in the top end of each leg, fitting the tenon to the slot. (*SEE FIGURES 8-4 AND 8-5.*)

5 Cut and drill the brace. Using a band saw, cut a taper in either end of the brace. It should decrease in thickness from ¾ inch near the center to ¼ inch at the ends, as shown in the *Side View.*

Drill the holes in the brace — a 1-inch-diameter hole to mount the brace to the pedestal, and four screw holes to mount the brace to the top. Make the four holes slightly larger than the shanks of the screws. This will allow the top to expand and contract with changes in humidity. Finally, countersink the screw holes.

> ## FOR BEST RESULTS
>
> **C**lamp each leg in a hand screw clamp and let the clamp ride along the top of the fence as you rout the tenon. This will help hold the leg in the proper position.

6 Turn the shape of the pedestal. Mount the pedestal on the lathe again and turn it to the shape shown in the *Pedestal Layout.* As you turn it, carefully fit the tenon at the top of the pedestal to the 1-inch-diameter hole in the brace. Finish sand the pedestal on the lathe.

8-2 Using an overarm router or an overhead routing jig (see "Making and Using an Overhead Routing Jig" on page 16), rout a dovetail slot in the bottom end of the pedestal stock. Loosen the straps, turn the stock 120 degrees, and rout another. Repeat until you have routed three slots, all ½ inch deep.

8-3 The dovetail tenons that fit these slots will have square shoulders. Because of this, you must cut a flat area on top of each slot. Remove the dovetail bit from the router and replace it with a ¾-inch straight bit. Rout the flats with the same setup you used to rout the slots. Square off the flats with a chisel. After you've cut the flats, the slots should be about ⅜ inch deep.

Remove the pedestal from the lathe. Using a band saw or a coping saw, cut two ⅛-inch-wide, ¾-inch-long slots in the tenon. These slots must be parallel to each other and perpendicular to one of the dovetail slots in the bottom end.

7 Rout the shape of the top. Mount a ¼-inch straight bit in your router, and mount the router in the *Large-Circle-Cutting Jig* shown on page 39. Use this jig to cut the round top.

8 Round-over the edges of the tabletop and legs. Remove the router from the jig and mount it in a router table. Replace the straight bit with a piloted ¼-inch quarter-round bit. Round-over the *top* edge of the tabletop. Switch to a piloted ½-inch quarter-round bit and roundover the *bottom* edge. This will create a thumbnail shape in the tabletop edge, as shown in the *Tabletop Section*.

Install a ⅜-inch roundover bit in the router and round-over the top edge of the legs, as shown in the *Leg Section*.

9 Assemble the candlestand. Finish sand all the parts you have made that still need it — legs, brace, and tabletop. Cut two wedges from a scrap of hardwood to fit the slots in the pedestal. Glue the brace to the pedestal, orienting the slots perpendicular to the length of the brace. Tap the wedges into the slots. When the glue dries, sand the wedges and the tenon flush with the top face of the brace.

Glue the legs in the dovetail slots at the bottom of the pedestal. When the glue dries, sand these joints clean and flush. Turn the tabletop and the pedestal assembly upside down and center the pedestal on the top. The brace should run perpendicular to the wood grain of the tabletop. Fasten the brace to the tabletop with screws (but *no* glue).

10 Finish the candlestand. Do any necessary touch-up sanding on the assembled candlestand, then apply a finish. The candlestand shown has been finished with a mixture of tung oil and varnish. Apply two coats of straight tung oil, letting each coat dry thoroughly. Mix two tablespoons of spar varnish into a cup of tung oil, and apply two more coats of this mixture. (The spar varnish makes the tung oil more durable and resistant to moisture.) Rub out the finish with paste wax and #0000 steel wool.

8-4 Cut the dovetail tenons in the legs with the *same* dovetail bit used to make the slots, installed in a table-mounted router. Cut each tenon in two passes — rout one face of the stock, turn it over, and rout the other face.

8-5 Slide each tenon into a mortise to test the fit. It should be snug, but not too tight. It's a good idea to rout several test tenons in scrap stock that's the same thickness as the legs and fine-tune your setup *before* routing the legs.

9

ROUTED BOX

Many early chests and boxes weren't joined or built up from boards. They were dug out from a single piece of wood. First, the craftsman split a section of a branch or a tree trunk along the long axis. Next, he used an adze and chisels to hollow out the larger of the split pieces and fit the smaller one to make a lid. As you might imagine, the task was long and laborious. But it produced some beautiful boxes with perfectly matched lids.

You can do the same thing on a smaller scale with a router. A routed box doesn't require nearly as much time and effort as a dug-out box, but the results can be just as exquisite.

There is no materials list for this project. You can make a routed box from almost any small block of wood. (Routing large boxes is impractical, since even the longest router bits won't cut more than 2 inches deep.) You can also glue up scraps, as I've done here, to make a single block from several woods of contrasting colors.

PLAN OF PROCEDURE

1 Select and prepare the stock. Select a block of straight-grained wood, no more than 2½ inches thick. (Don't use stock that is heavily figured or that has knots and other defects. The wood may come apart as you rout it.) You may want to glue up a block from smaller pieces. If you do, let the glue dry for *at least* 24 hours before routing the block.

2 Split the stock and rough-cut the shape of the box. Using a band saw or table saw, cut the block so the top part (or lid) is one-third to one-quarter of the total thickness, leaving the remainder for the bottom (or box). For example, if the block is 2 inches thick, saw a ³/₄-inch-thick top, and a 1¹/₄-inch-thick bottom.

Put the lid and box back together with double-faced carpet tape. Match the wood grains as if they were still a single block, and cut the parts in a rough circular shape, using a band saw or scroll saw. (*See Figure 9-1.*) Take the box and lid apart and discard the tape.

Using a compass, find the exact center of the *bottom* face of the lid and the *top* face of the box. Mark these centers, then drill a ⁵/₃₂-inch-diameter, ¹/₄-inch-deep hole at each mark. These holes will serve as the pivot points for the lid and the box.

3 Cut the lip in the lid. Mount a straight bit in a table-mounted router. Make the *Small-Circle-Cutting Jig* shown on page 39, and the *Router Jack* shown on page 11. Mount the circle-cutting jig on a router table and adjust its position to cut a circle whose radius (the distance from the pivot screw to the farthest edge of the bit) is about ¹/₄ inch smaller than the radius of the box. Place the router jack under the router and adjust the height of the bit just below the surface of the jig.

Place the box lid on the jig so the pivot hole fits over the pivot screw. Holding the lid firmly in place, turn on the router and raise the bit ¹/₈ inch. Slowly turn the lid counterclockwise, routing a circular groove in the bottom surface of the lid and leaving a ¹/₄-inch-wide lip all around the circumference. Raise the bit another ¹/₈ inch and rout the groove deeper. Repeat until the top of the bit is about ¹/₄ inch below the top surface of the lid.

Leave the router running. Loosen the bolt that holds the circle-cutting jig to the router fence and slide the jig (with the workpiece in place) about ¹/₈ inch closer to the bit. Tighten the bolt and make another cut, widening the groove. Repeat, removing more and more stock from the bottom surface of the lid. (*See Figure 9-2.*)

9-1 Split the wood block to make the box and lid, and cut them to a rough circular shape. If the block is large enough, don't split it completely. Leave about ½ inch uncut, as shown. This will eliminate the need to tape the parts together before cutting the circle.

9-2 Use the circle-cutting jig to cut a recess in the bottom surface of the lid. Remove most of the waste — all but a small knob in the center of the lid — by revolving the stock on the pivot.

Note: After you remove as much stock as you can, carefully measure how far the bit protrudes above the jig's worktable. You'll need this measurement when you rout the box.

When there's just a small knob left in the center of the lid, attach the lid to a scrap of plywood, using double-faced carpet tape. With a straight bit and an overarm router or an overhead routing jig (as described on page 16), cut away the knob in the center of the lid. (*SEE FIGURE 9-3.*) Remove the lid from the plywood and discard the tape.

4 Rout the rabbet on the edge of the box.
Readjust the circle-cutting jig to cut a small rabbet in the edge of the box. Adjust the depth of cut so the bit protrudes the same distance above the table as it did when you cut the recess in the lid — this will make the rabbet exactly as deep as the recess. To start, rout this rabbet only ¹/₁₆ inch wide, revolving the box on the pivot. Readjust the jig, moving the pivot another ¹/₁₆ inch toward the bit, and cut the rabbet a little wider. Repeat until the rabbet is as wide as the lip on the lid. (*SEE FIGURE 9-4.*) When completed, the lid should fit snugly (but not too tightly) over the rabbet.

5 Rout the recess in the box. Rout the recess in the box with the circle-cutting jig, using the same technique used to rout the lid. Rout a circular groove

¹/₄ inch inside the rabbeted edge of the box. Make this groove deeper and wider until there's just a knob left in the center of the box. Remove the knob with an overarm router or overhead routing jig.

6 Sand the box and lid to their finished diameter. Place the lid on the completed box. If it doesn't fit snugly, put a few strips of masking tape on the inside of the lip. The lid must fit tightly enough that you can't turn it easily. Using a disk sander, belt sander, or strip sander, sand both the box and the lid to their finished diameter. (*SEE FIGURE 9-5.*)

7 Finish the box. Finish sand the inside and outside of the box and lid. Apply a penetrating finish, such as tung oil or Danish oil, to all surfaces. (A finish that builds up on the surface, such as varnish or polyurethane, may interfere with the fit of the lid on the box.) When the finish dries, wax and buff both the inside and outside of the parts.

VARIATIONS

Instead of cutting the original block into a single box with a lid, split it into three or more parts to create a *stack* of boxes. Rout the bottom surface of each middle box to serve as a lid for the box beneath it.

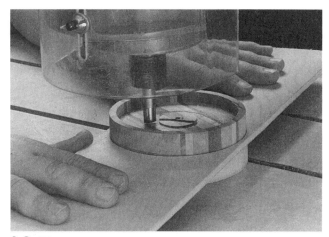

9-3 Use an overarm router or overhead routing jig to remove the knob in the center of the lid. For better control, attach the lid to a scrap of plywood. (This plywood should be somewhat larger than the lid.) Guide the lid freehand under the bit, being careful not to cut through the lip.

9-4 Using the circle-cutting jig, rout a rabbet in the top edge of the box. This rabbet should be as wide and as deep as the lip on the lid.

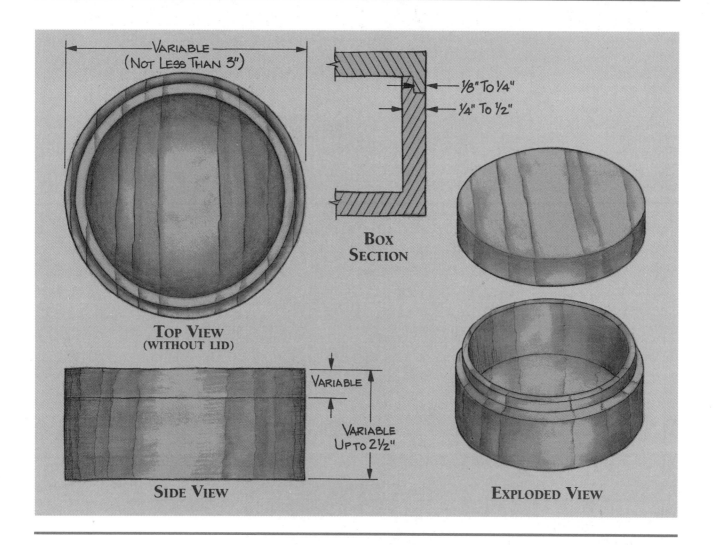

VARIABLE
(NOT LESS THAN 3")

BOX
SECTION

⅛" TO ¼"

¼" TO ½"

TOP VIEW
(WITHOUT LID)

VARIABLE

VARIABLE
UP TO 2½"

SIDE VIEW

EXPLODED VIEW

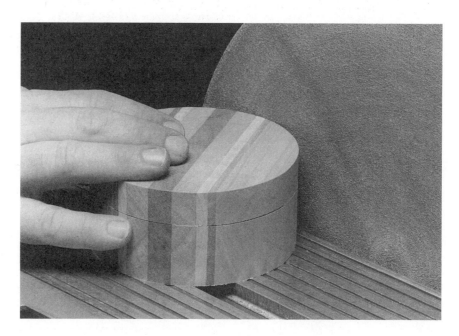

9-5 Sand the box and lid to their finished diameter, removing all saw and machine marks. Put the lid on the box as you sand to insure that both parts will be perfectly matched.

INDEX

Note: Page references in *italic* indicate photograph or illustration numbers. **Boldface** references indicate chapters.